Healing and Religious Faith

Healing and Religious Faith

CLAUDE A. FRAZIER, M.D., EDITOR

A PILGRIM PRESS BOOK

FROM UNITED CHURCH PRESS, PHILADELPHIA

Copyright © 1974 United Church Press
All Rights Reserved

No part of this publication may be reproduced, stored in a retrieval system, or transmitted in any form or by any means, electronic, mechanical, photocopying, recording, or otherwise, without the prior permission of the publisher.

Library of Congress Cataloging in Publication Data

Frazier, Claude Albee, 1920-
  Healing and religious faith.

  "A Pilgrim Press book."
  Includes bibliographical references.
  1. Faith-cure. I. Title. [DNLM: 1. Mental healing. 2. Religion and medicine. WB885 F848h]
BT732.5.F66   615'.852   74-13928
ISBN 0-8298-0276-2

Biblical passages marked NEB are from *The New English Bible, New Testament.* © The Delegates of the Oxford University Press and the Syndics of the Cambridge University Press, 1961. Reprinted by permission. Quotations marked TEV are from the Today's English Version of the New Testament. Copyright © American Bible Society 1966, 1971. Used by permission.

United Church Press, 1505 Race Street
Philadelphia, Pennsylvania 19102

CIP 2 3 OCT 1974

To a great nurse—Nina Francis Toney, R.N.—a great nurse in many ways.

Nina Francis Toney graduated from McKendree Hospital in Henton, West Virginia, in 1915 and nursed in the Robert Long Hospital of Indianapolis, Indiana, for about nine months. She did her private duty at Methodist Hospital in Indiana during the world influenza epidemic but also nursed in several other hospitals in the Indianapolis area.

While nursing her sister in St. Allons, West Virginia, she met and later married the attending physician. She helped her physician husband during his medical practice in the coalfields and told me many interesting stories about their early experiences there. She also cared for me and spent a great deal of time nursing me through my many illnesses.

Oh, yes, her married name is Mrs. Claude Frazier—my mother.

Contents

Foreword 7
BY NINA FRANCIS TONEY FRAZIER
Introduction 9
BY SISTER MARY JOSEPH BREWER, R.S.M.

I

1. Faith Healing 12
   BY GLENN R. FRYE, M.D.
2. Healing Miracles Today? 19
   BY BALFOUR M. MOUNT, M.D.

II

3. Life to the Dying 28
   BY CYNTHIA A. WHITE, R.N.
4. Religion and Faith Together 40
   BY DAVID JOHN ROCHE, R.N.
5. A Christian Attitude—Does It Make a Difference? 53
   BY DORIS V. DOUDS, R.N.
6. Faith, Thought, Feeling, and Healing 61
   BY FLORENCE R. DURKEE, R.N.
7. Faith Makes the Difference 70
   BY JUDITH CORRENTI, R.N.
8. Divine Physician 72
   BY IMOGENE KASERMAN, R.N.
9. Mighty Lourdes and Little Bernadette 76
   BY KARLA COOPER, R.N.
10. The Value of Christian Commitment in the Experiences of Stress and Illness 82
    BY MARGARET E. ARMSTRONG, R.N.
    AND JEAN MILLER, R.N.

III

11. Healing and Salvation: A Clinical View 94
    BY THE REV. ROBERT B. REEVES, JR.
12. Peeling the Healing Onion 105
    BY LOWELL H. MAYS
13. Spiritual Healing 113
    BY THE RT. REV. ALLEN W. BROWN
14. Hale and Hearty 118
    BY RABBI DAVID B. ALPERT
15. The Role of Religion and Faith in Facing Physical and Mental Illness and Death 131
    BY THE REV. GEORGE LEE GRAY
16. The Uniqueness of the Gospel in Healing 139
    BY THE REV. G. EDWARD BRYAN, PH.D.
17. The Relationship of the Human Spirit to the Holy Spirit in the Process of Healing 156
    BY THE REV. JOHN E. PENNINGTON, JR.
18. The Experience of Healing Prayer 164
    BY CANON H. L. PUXLEY
19. The Church's Ministry of Healing 175
    BY THE REV. EDWARD WINCKLEY, O.S.L.

Notes 182

Contributors 189

Foreword

BY NINA FRANCIS TONEY FRAZIER

I graduated from the McKendree General Hospital on June 22, 1915. Then I went to Robert Long Hospital in Indianapolis, Indiana, where I was in charge of obstetrics and the nursery. We often had four to five deliveries a day. Once I had to deliver a baby before the doctor could get to the delivery room; afterward, the doctor called me "Dr. Toney."

After nine months at Robert Long Hospital, I did private duty and had many patients at Methodist, St. Vincons, and Munie hospitals in Indianapolis and the surrounding area. I was also at Frankfort Hospital in Franklin, Illinois. In World War I, we converted a college into a hospital, and the professors and teachers all helped us. During this time there was an influenza epidemic. It was really awful! In 1916 I remember going to the train station to see sixty nurses leave to serve as war nurses in Europe. One died on the boat.

I was married in New York on June 22, 1918, and a few days later my husband, Dr. Claude Frazier, left for France. I continued to nurse one year following our marriage until his return to the States. He was originally from Knoxville, Tennessee. Just after his return we went to the coalfields in West Virginia. The miners were striking; as we went by the coal towns, rifles were stacked on the porches of the houses. We had a five-month-old son. It was an awfully wild place to live, but at least we did have water and heat in our house, which was more than some people had.

Our son had pneumonia frequently as a child and was often in the hospital, either at Charleston or Montgomery, West Virginia. Once when he had pneumonia at two years of age, I developed measles while nursing him. Just as he was recovering from pneumonia, he developed the measles. My husband and I thought he was a goner, but God answered our prayers and he lived. Later on several other occasions he was seriously ill, but God continued to hear our prayers and healed him. My husband

and I are strong believers in prayer and have seen God's answer to these prayers many times. Countless nights we have prayed most of the night, along with friends and relatives, for our sick child. We know that God answers prayer.

There were many interesting experiences during our years in the coalfields where my husband was the only doctor. I helped deliver babies. I took fish bones out of tonsils. I even delivered a baby once when my husband was out on another call. I helped my husband on night calls over cliffs and in shrubbery where there were bears or snakes around. I recall a miner threatening my husband's life. Once my husband saw one man shoot another and then dare my husband to go help the wounded man. He saw a young boy stab his father several times. He was threatened because a child died. It was a tough life then: the depression years, three children in school, no money. We saved a little and lost what we had. No one had any money to buy food, much less pay the doctor. My husband bought his own drugs to treat people. He walked for the first six years in practice before we had a car.

My husband never had more than one or two vacations in all that time. As many as five years would go by without his seeing his parents. If he ever left our house to go fourteen miles away to the drugstore, he would return to find a dozen patients on our porch demanding to know where he had been and insisting that he was needed immediately.

We were active in church from the early years of our marriage. I guess that was what brought us through those difficult years—our trust in God.

Introduction

BY SISTER MARY JOSEPH BREWER, R.S.M.

He has done it again! Another book to his credit and another gem for the enrichment of mankind. Claude Frazier is well equipped for the literary task he sets himself, for as a true Christian and as a physician he has had many opportunities to observe the role that religion and faith play in the healing process. Do you believe that there can be healing as a result of faith? What do the men and women whom Dr. Frazier has called upon have to say on the subject? Certainly they are also in a position to have witnessed the effects of faith at work.

In my twenty years of nursing, I have seen many times the truth of the supposition that faith can and does have a role in healing. But long before that, I was introduced to faith's healing qualities in my own person. Faith still enables me to surmount or at least counterattack the numerous physical, spiritual, and mental trials that beset us on the road of life.

What about miracles? Do you believe in their existence? I do. The whole of life is really a miracle. Can you look at a sunrise or sunset and doubt it? What about a raging ocean, whipped into fury by the tempestuous winds of a hurricane and yet confined within its own boundaries? Miraculous, to say the least. I remember a movie they showed in class one day when I was just a "probie" in nurses' training. Its goal, I think, was to instill in us a high regard for the value of life. It demonstrated man's inability to implant life in a grain of corn. Through his advanced intellectual and scientific powers, a scientist had duplicated a grain of corn so perfectly you could not distinguish his creation from a real grain, as far as appearances and texture went. But when both seeds were planted, only God's grain sprouted forth with new life; the grain of the scientist remained inert and lifeless where it had been placed. Life *is* a miracle! God has given man many powerful gifts—he has allowed man to be a partner with him in many ways—but he has retained for himself alone the role of life-giver. Parents may cooperate only so far in the production of their own offspring; it is only when God puts the breath of life into their united offering that it begins to develop and grow into a human being.

Can belief in miracles help a patient overcome his physical or mental illness? I believe it can. We should not *expect* God to work a miracle in our behalf, but I believe he can and will if, and whenever, he considers it wise to do so. Often we are blinded to God's miracles because we expect some grandiose performance rather than hidden, almost imperceptible, little things that are just as miraculous if our eyes of faith could but see. We rarely notice the most common miracle of all—that is, the numerous miracles of grace that take place around us almost every day. Each time we conquer our self is a genuine miracle, unseen by human eye but none the less real.

I hope Dr. Frazier's book may enable many who have hitherto been blind to open their eyes and see. Our God is omnipotent, powerful, wise, good, and all-knowing. Who is man to understand his unsearchable ways? And who is so bold as to dare to question the "whys and wherefores" of Almighty God? But just because I do not see with my eyes, or understand with my human intellect, does not eliminate the reality of the miracles that God can and does perform for millions of his children.

Faith brings peace; relaxation follows—these two promote more rapid healing. Faith believes against all odds and, believing, surmounts obstacles that before had seemed insurmountable. If I wanted to discredit or even discard faith completely, common sense would still argue that one who believes his suffering has a purpose and that God rules his destiny with love and wisdom has, as it were, an ace in the hole which, in turn, is conducive to a more prompt and complete healing than one who does not possess such belief. If faith can move mountains, how much more probable is the possibility that faith can promote healing in a body? It is wonderful to see a doctor big enough to believe in someone higher than himself and yet small enough to confess openly that belief. May God grant us an increase of such a noble tribe—which, in itself, would be no small miracle, believe me!

I

1

Faith Healing

BY GLENN R. FRYE, M.D.

At a meeting of the United Lutheran Church of America in convention in Dayton, Ohio, in 1958, the subject of healing by faith, sometimes known as spiritual healing or the art practiced by faith healers, was brought before the assembly. After considerable discussion, and when no conclusion could be reached, a motion was made to refer the subject to a committee. Later, the president of our church chose ten people to investigate the field of anointing and healing. I am one of them, together with three other doctors, five ministers, and one deaconess.

It might be well, first, for us to define spiritual or faith healing. We believe that God can and does heal. We believe that his healing power operates within the church but that it is not limited to the church; it includes the whole realm of the means of healing—medical science, psychiatry, and all other scientific methods that have been developed to heal the sick. Therefore, in speaking of faith healers we are talking about those individuals who claim they can heal by faith or prayer *alone* and deny that there are any other methods of curing the sick.

Physicians today no longer depend solely on medical and surgical means to restore health. We know that emotional upsets can produce physical symptoms. The physician and the clergyman are now cooperating more closely than ever before to overcome illness, whether it be physical or emotional. However, a faith healer has become known to the general public as an individual who claims that he can heal by faith alone. He does not cooperate with the medical profession. Such persons claim that medicine has no place in Christian life and behavior and that all things can be healed by prayer alone if the patient has sufficient faith. Thus, many spiritual healers have become the miracle men of the day. The promotional tactics they use are fantastic, and the incomes netted by some of these individuals in the name of religion have been astounding.

Some smaller sects believe in healing by prayer alone, but these are certainly not in the majority. The major bodies of Christendom believe that God's primary answer to the prayers and cries of suffering humanity comes through the service and skills of fellowmen—fellowmen who have been granted by God the compassion and intellect to discover some answers in their probing and searching for the prevention and relief of disease. We must never overlook the fact that in the history of the Christian Church a compassionate ministry to the body has always gone hand in hand with the ministry to the soul. With the church's gospel of good news for the future life have come hospitals, clinics, and the best medical skill of every century to offer the multitudes good news for the present also. It is most significant, I believe, that God chose Luke, a physician, as one of the Gospel writers and as historian of the early church.

However, there have often developed within the circle of the church unfounded hopes and misconceptions of the nature of healing. In the Church of Rome, for example, we find such places as the Lourdes shrine in France, the Fatima shrine in Portugal, the shrine of Saint Anne de Beaupré in Quebec, and other shrines of lesser importance. Thousands of people visit these places and hope for a miraculous recovery. There are probably a few documented cases of cures, but the percentage among the hundreds of thousands of people who go to these shrines is infinitesimally small. I am quite sure that most of the individuals who have thought they were cured and left their crutches behind have had to buy other pairs when they go home. However, we all know that the Roman Catholic Church does not claim to cure by faith alone, because no other religious body has as many hospitals throughout the world.

The theological basis for faith healing, of course, is taken from the New Testament, where many instances are recorded of Christ healing the sick and commanding his disciples to go and do likewise. Those who claim to heal by prayer alone would make you believe that Christ meant prayer to be the only basis for healing and that the science of medicine had nothing to do with it. When you look into the history of medicine, you find that its practice in the centuries following the birth of Christ was indeed very crude. Man had neither much knowledge of disease nor the means to treat it. Today it is a different story.

Probably more progress has been made in the past fifty years in the scientific understanding of the causes and treatment of disease than in the two thousand years before that. Today such scourges as typhoid fever, smallpox, yellow fever, and epidemic plague have been practically wiped out. This has been accomplished by discovering the causes, cures, and prevention of these diseases. So far as the surgical field is concerned, we now cure patients by performing operations that were impossible even a few years ago. And when one thinks of miracles, what about the miracle drugs? Penicillin alone has saved hundreds of thousands of lives since its discovery. In just one disease, pneumonia, the death rate has dropped from 30 percent to practically nothing. When we think of these things—and when we think of little children who are being spared permanent crippling disability through the use of polio vaccine—we can only bow and thank God for these miracles. The ingredients for all these drugs have been here since the beginning of time; it is only through the knowledge that was given man by the Lord when he created him that man has been able to make these discoveries and produce these drugs and effect these cures that are miracles in themselves.

I would not want to be misunderstood. I have faith that miracles can be performed today in healing the sick just as they were in the days when Christ was on earth. But the question comes up and is one we must answer: Is that God's plan of healing? Is it his plan that all healing should be by faith alone and nothing by the works of man? Was it never intended for man to make these discoveries and produce these miracles of healing? I hope that we cannot support that negative theory. No sensible individual would claim that all these things should be disregarded, or that all one needs to do is pray to be cured of an illness. Let me hasten to say that prayer is essential in the cure of any patient and a patient who has a firm Christian belief will often get well quicker than the nonbeliever. On the other hand, many patients who are nonbelievers and non-Christian get well just as readily as Christian ones. I do not believe the theory that all illness and sickness is brought on as punishment for sins we have committed. At the same time, it is quite true that certain diseases are caused by intemperate and immoral living.

If one believes that the miracles which Christ performed on earth are all to be interpreted as the pattern we should follow in the years to come, what about the miracles of the feeding of the five thousand, the changing of water into wine, and many others? Does it mean that all we need to do now is to pray for our daily bread as we do when we say in the Lord's Prayer, "Give us this day our daily bread"? Do these individuals who claim they can heal by prayer alone believe that they can have daily bread by prayer alone also? In my opinion, one is just as logical as the other. When we pray for our daily bread we really pray for rain, sunshine, good soil, and the ability to earn our living. We know that the methods of tilling the soil used in early days could not feed the hundreds of millions of people now living on earth, any more than the type of medicine practiced in those days could effect cures for the millions of people in today's dense population. The research in agronomy which has enabled us to produce more food on the same acreage has paralleled the research in medicine which has enabled us to lower the death rate of our population. The two can be classed as parallel achievements, but so far I have not heard of any faith feeders as we have heard of faith healers.

One of the functions of the committee which was appointed by the United Lutheran Church was to investigate the cures alleged to have been made at different shrines or by different individuals who claim they cure by prayer alone. Let me say in the first place that it is very difficult to prove any of these claims. There are many testimonials to be read today, but one is struck by their similarity to those testimonials of yesterday for Lydia Pinkham's Vegetable Compound and Doan's Kidney Pills. They make claims which I do not think can be true. For instance, one of Oral Roberts' converts was a woman who said that the doctors had "given her up" and could not cure her; she had rheumatism and diabetes and one leg was shorter than the other. Then, she claimed, after one prayer session, her diabetes was gone, her rheumatism had disappeared, and the one leg had grown to the same length as the other. The truthfulness of these claims, of course, cannot be proved. However, there are some cases on record of people who have been cured and apparently cured by faith after all other means had failed. This, I grant, is quite possible, because the Lord can cure anyone he wishes to cure, but the fact that a few have been cured by faith alone is in no way to be taken that that is the only way the Lord meant for healing to be done. If that were true, why would he have put all the resources here that man has found and utilized so successfully in his search for the treatment and cure of disease? If faith alone is the Lord's plan of healing, why would he have made all these other things available? I do not believe that the knowledge and skill and scientific research of the medical profession exist without God's favor.

One cannot help but be struck by the similarity of the claims of the faith healers in religion and those of the quack healers in medicine. One has only to look down through the long history of quacks in medicine to see a parallel to the faith healers of religion. Crowds flock to them just as they flock to faith healers. Many people will believe anything, no matter how fantastic, when it concerns their health. These quacks vary in their methods, but they all ignore the science of medicine, deny the germ theory, and do not believe in antibiotics. By one special procedure or another, they claim to cure all diseases.

One woman claimed she could cure any disease by merely rubbing the limb of an apple tree with one hand and laying her other hand on the patient's head. She kept this up for many months. The crowds became so great they had to camp nearby the night before in order to get in line the next day. Eventually, disillusionment came and the crowds thinned, but nevertheless her bank account grew larger. Then there are those who claim that they can take one drop of blood on a slide and put it into a special machine and give you a diagnosis from the number of lights that flash on the machine. One of these quacks got along very well until someone sent him a drop of blood taken from a young rooster and he sent back the diagnosis: This patient has cancer and tuberculosis and is three months pregnant. After that his practice dwindled.

Then there is another group known as the cancer quacks. They claim they have a cure for cancer, and thousands flock to them. Of course, these people are not cured, but they spend fantastic sums of money taking one treatment or another. The financial loss is nothing compared with the bitter disillusionment and heartache when the patient realizes that nothing has been accomplished. The same is true of the faith healer who promises to cure and gets his followers into such an emotional state that they sometimes think they are well but after this state subsides they are bitterly disappointed to find they are still in the same condition as they were in the beginning. Then there are those who go long distances and wait in line to be prayed over or touched, hoping to have a cure, and are so ill they may die before they return home. These examples show us the similarity between the faith healer and the quack medicine man.

One of the things that impresses me about some of the faith healers and their instruction concerns how to organize prayer teams. One of the most prominent ones suggests that there should not be less than six or more than twelve on the team that goes to pray. The time of prayer with the patient should not be less than thirty minutes or over an hour. Now, I am a firm believer in prayer and I think many of our prayers are answered if they are not too selfish, but nowhere in the Bible, to my knowledge, does it say how many shall pray or how long they shall do so to get the Lord to answer. The thief on the cross said, "Lord, remember me when thou comest into thy kingdom." Christ answered, "To day shalt thou be with me in paradise (Luke 23:42-43)." In the organization of these prayer teams into certain numbers of people and certain hours of prayer, the concept would seem to be that if one prays long enough, and with enough people, one can force the Lord to answer one's prayers.

Another reason to study faith healing is the fact that many pastors are asking what they shall do about faith healing. Some of their members are asking them why the church does not have special services for healing the sick, similar to those carried on by the faith healers. Many churches of various denominations have these kinds of services. I want to emphasize that I am not speaking of this form of worship. I am not speaking about the churches that have prayer for the sick or special services for them. These services are not carried out with the thought of healing by faith alone, but the churches recognize the part the medical profession plays in it and they advise that all of these things be made available to the individual who is ill. They recognize that healing the sick depends on medical science—physicians, nurses, technicians, and other members of the medical team—and that prayer is an adjunct and is not intended to be the only method used. Many of the denominations have had committees who have studied this subject, but so far as I am able to ascertain none of these committees has made a report advising that prayer and prayer alone should be used in healing the sick.

I want to reemphasize the importance of the role I think the church plays in healing the sick and pay tribute to pastors for the help they give to physicians. It has finally begun to dawn on the members of the two professions that they should depend on each other. What may come as a new thought to some of you is that a strong Christian faith may materially aid in restoring health, even in case of organic illness, and that, where health cannot be restored, faith can make the remainder of the life in question as productive and happy as possible. In cases where the only prospect is for complete invalidism, suffering, and certain death, a strong faith can make this acceptable and thus preserve the patient's emotional and mental health. We realize that probably 50 percent of the patients we see have no organic illness. We know that fear, hostility, insecurity, and guilt can be the source of the trouble and be expressed by physical symptoms. It is in these emotional types of illness that the pastor can be of the greatest service.

Some emotional and functional illnesses can be cured rather quickly if the pastor can encourage the sufferers to develop a strong Christian faith. However, there are others who must have counseling over a long period of time and have someone in whom they trust and in whom they are willing to confide. Their minister or the chaplain in the hospital is most likely to be that individual. The minister recognizes that his own ministration may facilitate the task of the physician and that the work of the physician may contribute to the spiritual well-being of the patient. Healing is, therefore, seen as the proper use of all God-given measures by a number of persons in different walks of life.

2

Healing Miracles Today?

BY BALFOUR M. MOUNT, M.D.

Stan, a shrewd internist whose steadfast Christian faith was born in a prisoner-of-war camp in Japan, was deeply concerned about one of his patients, a widely respected businessman, father, church leader, and friend. He had severe acute glomerulonephritis, and his condition was rapidly deteriorating in spite of optimal care. As a joint act of desperate faith, those who were close to the case, family and physician, met for prayer. The results were startling. Immediately, the course of the glomerulonephritis changed and the patient's condition stabilized, then rapidly improved. The flow sheet documenting laboratory parameters of disease reflected a clear-cut turning point in the pathologic process. That turning point coincided temporarily with the time when two or three gathered together in his name (Matthew 18:20).

Was it a present-day miracle? If a second patient had the same serious problem but improved without prayer, would that be a miracle? If we could explain in medical terms why the patient improved, would that explain away the miracle or would it still be a miracle?

A man with kidney cancer has tumor spread to his lungs and much to the amazement of all he suddenly has a "spontaneous regression"; the disease simply disappears. A miracle? We now know that the cure can be explained by his own bodily defense mechanisms and the immune system; his body has been successful in rejecting the cancer. Does that mean we need not resort to the word miracle to explain the event? Does God ever use immunologic means to accomplish his ends? We have passed the old historic trap of finding evidence for God only in things we cannot understand, so that God appears to become less relevant as our knowledge increases. If there is a God, he surely does not depend on our ignorance for his security. The role of the church in each generation is to reexamine Christ and his meaning with every new light and instrument available. To do so may be to begin to understand some of God's miracles, but our understanding does not undermine his authorship.

The area of faith healing and miracles seems unsettling to many of us today, and yet we must consider it with care because miracles are an essential part of Jesus' story. For example, material dealing with miracles comprises 30 percent (209 verses out of 666) of Mark's Gospel. Furthermore, Christ's comments in the area seem clear: "Ask, and you will receive (Matt. 7:7, NEB)"; "Whatever you pray for in faith you will receive (Matt. 21:22, NEB)"; "Indeed anything you ask in my name I will do (John 14:13, NEB)." Yet the English word miracle is not used at all in the *Revised Standard Version* of the New Testament, while in the *King James Version* it appears only twice in the first three Gospels. The early writers preferred such words as "power, sign, mighty work."

Perhaps, then, a reexamination of the word "miracle" is in order. One dictionary defines miracle as "an event that appears to be neither a part nor a result of any known natural law or agency and is therefore often attributed to a supernatural or divine source." This definition clearly refers to that area characterized by man's ignorance, and we may expect fewer and fewer "miracles" of this sort as the information explosion continues. Perhaps what we need for the twenty-first century is a new definition. I like this one: "Miracles are signs of God's intervention in human affairs through which believers can come to see deep truths regarding Jesus."

The Miracles of Jesus

If we consider the first-century miracles of Jesus, we will find documentation of real people coming to him with real illnesses and specific complaints. A pattern is noted. Jesus heals them with a word or physical act. Their total cure is signified by a word or physical act, and those who are witnesses are greatly affected. There is definite evidence that he avoided the sensational, frequently cautioned against telling others, and both refused to give a demonstration of miracles (Mark 8:12) and suggested that it was wrong to look for such a demonstration (1 Corinthians 1:22). Clearly, these acts were meant to stand as evidence of God's love even as his life among us was.

Several explanations have been advanced by skeptics to explain the miracles of Jesus.

1. They simply did not occur as historical events.

2. Christ healed psychosomatic ills by the power of suggestion.

3. Ordinary happenings became magnified as the stories were passed from generation to generation to become miraculous.

4. Christ simply made use of a superior knowledge of medicine, and with progress in the medical sciences his miracles will be quite understandable.

There is little to support the first thesis. It seems clear from all accounts that *something* happened on numerous occasions and that Christ was the instrument in some way for the relief of suffering. The sad aspect of the remaining three theses is that although they each may contain an element of truth they all completely miss the issue. By looking so hard at the *how*, they miss the *why*. By throwing up windmills to joust at, they miss the message. The significant feature is not how they happened; the marvel is that they did happen and that they changed people's lives and gave them fresh insights into God's love.

Miracles Today

What evidence is there for modern healing miracles? The documentation is as varied as are the sources: unexplained medical findings from the charts of private physicians, Boards of Inquiry into the healing phenomena at national shrines such as Lourdes, the books and TV programs of personalities such as Katherine Kuhlman and Oral Roberts.

One cannot live in airtight compartments, and so twentieth-century man tends to approach these data as he does all other aspects of experience, analytically and skeptically. Conditioned by his mistrust of Madison Avenue, he believes half of what he sees and less of what he hears. A product of Alvin Toffler's 800th generation and the age of future shock, he is self-sufficient, with little place for things lacking proof and less room for faith. In spite of this bias which we all share to a varying extent, I must conclude that as far as I am concerned: (1) the quality of love revealed in the first-century miracles is completely consistent with continuing similar events today; (2) men and women I know convince me that the power of Christ is alive and well and living in their lives, and thus I can believe that all things are possible; (3) I have not personally experienced an unexplainable healing miracle; (4) I have personally experienced God's intervention in the presence of illness to relieve suffering and, in so doing, his revealing new insights to those involved; (5) miracles represent a fulfillment and not a contravention of natural law.

Regarding the unexplainable healing miracles, I accept that they may occur but cannot feel that this is God's usual modus operandi. It brings to mind Bill Cosby's skit "Noah" in which Noah is admonished for having two male hippos on the ark and shouts to the Lord, "Why don't you change one of them?"—to which the Lord replies, "You know I don't work like that!" Although I believe it possible, I just don't think the Lord usually works like that.

What then do we pray for? "Whatever you pray for in faith you will receive." Do we pray therefore, in faith, for sunny days, new cars, and good health and receive them? Are there limits, or can the faithful call on God as a divine diddler in their affairs? Does he require some discernment on our part? Does he ask us to add, "Not as I will, but as thou wilt (Matt. 26:39)"? Are we to keep in mind as well that "Your Father knows what your needs are before you ask him (Matt. 6:8, NEB)"? The matter is not simple. Let us pray in humility to be cured, perhaps, but let us pray first for his presence, support, comfort, and strength. Tom Dooley's third book, *The Night They Burned the Mountain*, was written after he knew he was dying of cancer. As we read, our eyes meet the steady gaze of an Irishman who knew the Lord, a gaze that is unwavering in the face of progressive illness. You come away with the distinct feeling that he knew how to pray!

There are further aspects of this faith-healing brand of miracles that bother me. What of the family members who are estranged and bitter after the death of their small child from leukemia. Who needed more faith, the child or the parents? If only their faith had been greater, "Whatever you pray for in faith you will receive." What of the patient who is gravely ill and prays in faith for a cure only to have his illness progress? He has several dangers: losing confidence in his faith, losing confidence in God, withdrawing from his relationship with Christ and losing the great potential for peace, and delaying or compromising medical investigations, therapy, and follow-up in a swirl of hope.

A further pitfall which we must try to understand in this setting is the prayer, "Thy will be done." What greater prayer is there? It was taught to us by Christ, spoken by him at Gethsemane, and yet what does it mean in this setting of suffering? Does the young husband lose his wife in childbirth and pray, "Thy will be done"? Do thousands die in Pakistan at the hand of nature's violence and pray, "Thy will be done"? Does God will the agonizing death of the cancer patient or the torment of mental illness? For many it is easier to think of a world without a creator than of a creator loaded with all the contradictions of the world. Caught in this problem, we may hear the faithful say with regard to suffering, "God has willed it, so it must be for the good. It is difficult to understand now, but there is a reason." I cannot accept this. God does not *will* suffering, although he may utilize suffering in many ways and one frequently grows spiritually through the process. The question of faith healing is thrown into prominence by the mysteries of the problems of suffering in a world that we are to believe is under the control of a good God. As part of the answer we may turn to rigid doctrines and to faith healing, only to be left with the above problems, or we may be forced to conclude as Archibald MacLeish did in *J.B.*, "If God is God he is not good; if God is good he is not God." The Rev. Jim Crawford, who worked for some time in East Harlem, said after reflecting on the struggles, hardships, and disasters which mark the lives of so many that it is difficult to find conclusive evidence of a benevolent loving God in history, in nature, or in the events of individual lives, for if we find an example of his apparent presence in one of these areas in one instance we will find his apparent absence in another instance. The conclusive evidence lies not in history, nature or the events of lives but in the fact of Jesus Christ. The basic question is not "What do you think of suffering?" but "What do you think of the Christ?" Having answered the second question, we may turn to the first in confidence and say in faith, "I just don't know. I *do* know, though, where to go with the problem." Let us pray, then, "Thy will be done," and look for evidence of his modern-day miracles not only in the beneficial turn of events we cannot understand and explain but also in the wonder of his presence and support, in increasing medical knowledge regarding the etiology and pathogenesis of disease, and in increasing expertise in treating the suffering patient.

One gray November day as I came swimming back from the abyss of anesthesia I heard the words, "You did have a malignant tumor, Bal, an embryonal carcinoma." In the ensuing years my path has been such that the surgical and medical treatment of these tumors has occupied much of my clinical and research time. From a vantage point of several years I can say as an investigator and clinical oncologist that I am probably cured of my disease and that the cure was predictable with a high degree of probability immediately following pathologic staging of the tumor. I was cured because the cancer was caught early. To simplify what happened in that way, however, is to miss the real meaning that the event had and continues to have for me. In working through the realities of having a malignancy, and accepting a life span of less than eighteen months, I came face to face with Christ. It is fascinating now to go back over those events and see how I received concrete support through each of the steps toward acceptance of my tumor. Elisabeth Kübler-Ross in documenting these steps for both the patient and his relatives has shown that they include denial, anger, the phase of asking "Why me?" the phase of bargaining, and the phase of acceptance. In each stage the road was opened for me and the obstacles cleared by Jesus Christ, through the lives, words, and actions of people, places, and books around me. John Fitzgerald Kennedy, who had been assassinated only days before; Marian Anderson, whose presence always reflects his presence; Tom Dooley, whose calm acceptance of malignancy allowed staggering productivity in his remaining months; a hospital chapel with his words enscribed on its walls, "Come unto me, all ye that labor and are heavy laden, and I will give you rest (Matt. 11:28)"; friends who taught me the meaning of koinonia and the brotherhood of the church as they prayed for me. Was my cure a miracle? For me it was, since it helped me to see God. That a powerful ally is standing ready to aid in time of need was made clear to me. A day or two after the first operation, I lay alone in the hospital room. Well, Lord, I remember thinking in desperation, this is really it. If you are really there, if there is any basis for faith, now is the time to put it on the line. Let's hear it. I was frightened, depressed, and alone. Picking up the hospital bedside Bible, I let it open at random, the challenge still in my mind. In wonderment I started to read Psalm 116, a passage I had never previously read:

> I love the Lord, because he has heard
> > my voice and my supplications.
> Because he inclined his ear to me,
> > therefore I will call on him as long as I live.
> The snares of death encompassed me;
> > the pangs of Sheol laid hold on me;
> > I suffered distress and anguish.
> Then I called on the name of the Lord:
> > "O Lord, I beseech thee, save my life!"
>
> Gracious is the Lord, and righteous;
> > our God is merciful.
> The Lord preserves the simple;
> > when I was brought low, he saved me.
> Return, O my soul, to your rest;
> > for the Lord has dealt bountifully with you.
> For thou hast delivered my soul from death,
> > my eyes from tears,
> > my feet from stumbling;
> I walk before the Lord
> > in the land of the living.
> I kept my faith, even when I said,
> > "I am greatly afflicted";
> I said in my consternation,
> > "Men are all a vain hope."
>
> What shall I render to the Lord
> > for all his bounty to me?
> I will lift up the cup of salvation
> > and call on the name of the Lord,
> I will pay my vows to the Lord
> > in the presence of all his people.
> Precious in the sight of the Lord
> > is the death of his saints.
> O Lord, I am thy servant;

> I am thy servant, the son of thy handmaid.
> Thou hast loosed my bonds.
> I will offer to thee the sacrifice of thanksgiving
> and call on the name of the Lord.
> I will pay my vows to the Lord
> in the presence of all his people,
> in the courts of the house of the Lord,
> in your midst, O Jerusalem.
> Praise the Lord!

Should you ask me, "Do you believe in healing miracles?" I would have to answer "yes." Perhaps, though, we would have to explore what each of us understands by those two words and then be prepared to stand in ignorance of the absolute truth which is his understanding.

II

3
Life to the Dying

BY CYNTHIA A. WHITE, R.N., B.S., M.A.

A person could have all the faith in the world in a bright red umbrella—so much faith as to go to the top of the Empire State Building, open the umbrella, and jump. But his tremendous faith in that bright red umbrella would not save him from being killed when he hits the ground. It is not how much faith we have but in whom we have our faith.

Serious illness and impending death will often cause people to reveal their true concept of God. "God's punishing me" (God as the policeman). "Why is God letting this happen? I have gone to church all my life, given lots of money to the church, and tried to be good" (God as the one to be bought or bargained with). There are many other possibilities along this line, but these are enough to make a point. Often, our relationship with God is uni-directional—what God can do to or for us. It is this one-sided faith that can defeat us when we are confronted with reverses in life. A uni-directional relationship with God often brings greater destruction to the patient in the hospital (and to his family) than the physical disease he has.

There are many definitions of faith. Webster's dictionary gives several; one is "complete trust, confidence or reliance," as children usually have faith in their parents. The book of Hebrews in the New Testament devotes all of chapter 11 to faith telling how, "by faith," several of the men from the Old Testament were able to do the impossible or go through impossible trials. "But faith forms a solid ground for what is hoped for, a conviction of unseen realities (Heb. 11:1, BERKELEY)." As one reads the story of Abraham's being asked to sacrifice his only son Isaac (Genesis 22), the only explanation of Abraham's being able to obey is that he had complete trust in God. In verse 8 Abraham says, "God will provide."

One Friday, I was asked to see a patient whose life depended on an artificial kidney. She was only forty-two years old and had three teen-age children. She told me she didn't want to die, and as we talked she mentioned God and said she didn't have much faith. I looked at her and said, "You know, we read in the Bible about how people were able to go through such trials, and we think, 'Oh, but they were different; they were stronger, they were closer to God.' But really, the only difference between these people and you and me is that they really knew the Person in whom they had their faith. Paul and Silas, in Acts 16, were thrown in jail and bound, and we read: 'About midnight, Paul and Silas were praying and singing hymns to God (Acts 16:25).' This is a very unusual response to potential disaster. They didn't know what their future held—they could be killed—and the only reason they were able to do this was because they knew what God was like, not because they were special. They trusted that God would work this to good, even if they couldn't see how." This patient was transferred to another hospital, but my prayer for her is that she will, through reading scripture and praying, find out what God is like for herself.

A modern-day example of the above can be found in Corrie Ten Boom's book *The Hiding Place*.[1] Corrie and her sister Betsie were in a German concentration camp as a result of harboring Jews in their home in Holland. They found themselves in a flea-infested barracks. Betsie's response to this was a prayer of thanksgiving for the fleas; Corrie's was that this could not be of God. They found out later that, because of the fleas, theirs was the only barracks not visited by the guards, and this gave them complete freedom to hold prayer meetings and Bible studies. Fleas—a gift from God?

How can we help those who are faced with death? In a book on the Christian attitude toward death, *The View from a Hearse*, Joe Bayly shares some of what he and his wife and family have been through when confronted with death.[2] Joe and Mary Lou watched three sons die—John, eighteen days old; Danny, five years old; and Joe, Jr., eighteen years old. Joe talks about death as a complete separation from the world as we know it and a "journey through a tunnel." He likens it to the physical process of birth. We so often see death as only a negative. We fear it because of the separation it brings. We can only deal with its reality if we believe that God's promise of eternal life to those who receive life in Jesus Christ is truth.

A patient was dying of cancer, and she was very depressed. She said in answer to "What comes after this life?" that she believed she would just sleep for eternity. I prayed with her daily, and she began reading the New Testament. One day she said, "I now have no place to go but to Jesus." Another patient said she didn't want to die "because you're dead so long—my father died when he was forty-three, and he has now been dead longer than he lived." She was told that there was a book that told how we could have life after death (the New Testament), and her response was, "Get me that book." Both these patients began to live as they were dying. "But faith forms a solid ground for what is hoped for, a conviction of unseen realities."

Why do we have to die? Just a short time ago, this question was asked me by the nursing staff caring for a forty-year-old woman who was dying of cancer. She was leaving behind three children and a mentally ill husband. She was also leaving behind a mother who had undergone bilateral radical mastectomies for breast cancer and a father who had a colostomy for bowel cancer. This woman's twenty-nine-year-old sister and thirty-two-year-old brother had both died of cancer within the past two years. The patient had been in a coma for four days, and her mother had not left the bedside. Besides asking "Why?" the staff also asked, "How can you present a God of love in light of what this family has gone through?" My initial reaction was to run. I felt trapped by this question. As I sat there, praying for God's wisdom, the second and third chapters of Genesis came to mind. The following paragraph is basically what I shared with them.

"In the second chapter of Genesis, we have the Creation as it was originally meant to be. God created the heavens and the earth and all the things in them. Then God created man and breathed into man his breath, 'and man became a living soul (Gen. 2:7),' and God created woman. Adam's response to God was perfect harmony, as was Eve's. Their response to each other and to the earth was also perfect harmony. The only limitation put on their lives was that they were not to eat of the tree of the knowledge of good and evil. Then we look at the third chapter, and we see a picture of today. Everything is in a turmoil, and disharmony is all that is present. What happened? Temptation came on the scene. The serpent brought temptation. First he said, So, you can't eat any fruit from any tree? to which Eve answered, Oh, no, we can eat from all but the one in the center of the garden. If we eat from that one, we shall surely die. (This is a spiritual, not physical, death.) The serpent then said, Oh, you won't die; God just doesn't want you to eat from that tree because you would know good and evil and be like him. So Eve took a bite and gave it to Adam (and we don't see anywhere that Adam argued with her), and everything blew! Fear came into their hearts, especially fear of God, and they hid when they heard him coming. When God confronted them with their disobedience, Adam's immediate response was to pass the buck. He even blamed God for what happened. 'The woman whom thou gavest to be with me, she gave me fruit of the tree, and I ate (Gen. 3:12).' First we blame God and then someone else. We are no different today, and what we experience today is a direct result of what happened in the third chapter. It has been multiplied over the years by our continuing to disobey God. What this family is going through is not a punishment for something they have done; it is the result of universal sin. 'All have sinned and fall short of the glory of God (Rom. 3:23),' and all this will continue until all are reborn. This is what Jesus is talking about in John 3. Flesh begets flesh. If you are born, you are a physical being; you have no choice in this. But you do have a choice about remaining only flesh. You can choose to accept the spiritual birth offered to us through Jesus Christ's having died for each one of us and his resurrection. This you do by choice, consciously asking Jesus to be Lord and Savior of your life. It is only through this experience of being reborn that you will ever be any different than you are today."

The next evening when I came on duty, the head nurse on that floor told me the patient was still alive. She said she couldn't understand it. I told her I couldn't understand it either, but I knew there was a purpose because God does not waste anything. I went to that floor about 5 P.M. and looked into the room. This was the first time the mother was alone. I entered and sat down next to her and said, "It hurts, doesn't it?"

She said, "Yes, and I can't bring myself to leave. I keep waiting for the silence."

So often, when I find myself in this kind of situation, I ask the Lord to keep me from making things harder for people. I finally spoke again. "You know, I've left here four nights now, and every time I've left, I've asked God why you are having to go through this. It has also been a burden on my heart that you may in some way be blaming yourself for the death of your children."

She looked surprised and then said, "Yes, I have. I've wondered if I breast-fed them too long, or gave them the wrong food, or took them to the wrong places. I suppose if I believed in God the way I did when I was twelve, I would be wondering if God was punishing me for something."

The Lord enabled me to respond with, "No, God is not vindictive. He is hurting with you every minute that you are suffering. I know he cares about what you're going through because he has given me a concern for you. The only reason I'm in this room with you right now is because he loves you and wants you to know that." At this point I told her about the question the staff had asked the night before, and the reply that I had given.

When I finished, she said, "Yes, we have made a mess of this world, and we continue to." Then I prayed with her and left. Her daughter died two hours later.

When a patient accepts the reality of impending death and has come to grips with the reality of Jesus Christ and knows him as Savior and Lord, a real sense of freedom is present. We had a patient who had been in and out of a hospital for a year with leukemia. She was in her fifties and had walked many years with Jesus Christ. She fought just as hard as the next person to stay alive—the will to live is God-given—but when she learned that there were no more medications and no more treatments available, her response to the doctor was, "I'm not afraid to die, as I know I will be with Jesus in the kingdom. If you can give me something to relieve the pain, I would appreciate it. If not, I will trust God to give me the grace to bear it." This woman's faith resulted in the head nurse's calling her whole staff together after she died. They had a time of prayer, in which they thanked God for what this patient had taught them and asked him to help them help other patients with what they had learned.

Why do we fear death? We try so hard to postpone it, even to the point of having machines carry out all the human vital functions. We see today a new way of denying its reality in the freezing of the dead bodies and relatives visiting the "deep freeze" and viewing the body of their dead loved one on a regular basis. (There is one of these facilities on Long Island.) It is this fear which keeps us from being able to talk with or listen to the dying person. It is this fear that makes me do all the talking—mainly about trivia—and keeps me from just sitting down and saying to the patient, "What's on your heart?" It is this fear that drives me to try to control things in every way so that the patient cannot get through my protective shield and involve me in his dying.

The first thing we have to deal with, before we can really hang in there with the dying patient, is our own fear of death. And the only healthy way this is possible is through a greater awareness and understanding of who God is and what he is like. God doesn't want to beat us to a pulp, smash us, or torture us. He wants to make us whole. To the extent to which we begin to see that God really does care (Psalm 139 is a strong argument that he does), and become aware of his Presence, to that extent we will be free not to fear. One of the modern translations of the Bible gives a very gut-level twenty-third Psalm. "The Lord is my shepherd; I have everything I need. . . . He gives me new strength. He guides me in the right way, as he has promised. Even if that way goes through deepest darkness, I will not be afraid, Lord, because you are with me (vv. 1, 3-4, TEV)." Those of us who are Christians so often say truth with our heads only. "Perfect love casts out fear (1 John 4:18)" is an example of this. It is only through *experiencing* the deep love of God, through reading his Word and believing that his Word is truth, that his love can touch us and others through us.

How do we help someone who is dying? What do we have to offer?

A young man named Tom, nineteen years old, an only child, was admitted to the hospital in July. Diagnosis: leukemia. Tom was about to enter his third year of college. The staff asked me to come and see Tom because they were too close to his age, and his disease would probably result in death, and they wanted an "uninvolved" person. The first morning Tom and I just chatted about his summer job and his plans for school. Then he turned away from me and pretended to go to sleep. I sat there for a time and then, as I was leaving, told him I would be back the next day. The next day Tom made a pass at me (though I'm old enough to be his mother), and when I parried it, he said, "I didn't think you'd go for that." On the third day Tom began to talk about having leukemia and what his chances were. This taught me something about investment. Tom knew what he had. He knew it could result in death. His testing was apparently for the purpose of finding out if I would really hang in there with him. When you're dying, you can't afford to invest in a relationship where the other person will duck out when the going gets rough. The best way to find out is to try to chase them away or turn them off.

One evening, when Tom's white blood count was almost nothing and everyone who entered his room had to wear gowns and masks to protect Tom from infection, Tom said, "I wish they would stop the protection so I could get a bug and kick the bucket."

The Lord enabled me to respond with, "The only trouble with that, Tom, is that you might not get a bug bad enough to kill you. It might just make you sicker."

He looked a bit surprised and then said, "Oh, I hadn't thought of that."

It would have been so easy to have given one of the usual "turn-off" responses such as "Oh, you shouldn't talk like that" or "You don't want to die" or "We're doing what's best for you"—all of which really say "Don't talk about dying because it makes me uncomfortable."

How do we help someone who is dying? We help by believing that the Lord cares more for this person than we do and that the Lord will give the right words at the right time, by trusting that he knows this person better than we do, by being willing to be the vessel of God's love to this person, by believing that the Lord will meet our needs so that we in turn will be free to meet the needs of this person—and a dying person's greatest need is to know that there is someone who will go as far as the door of death with him.

After some time, Tom found out that one of my interests in nursing was the spiritual needs of patients. The evening this came out, it looked as though our friendship might hit the rocks because Tom was a confessed atheist. But the friendship was solid by that time, and instead of backing off, Tom said, "You know, I was brought up an atheist, and before tonight I never considered another alternative. What is God like?"

How do you answer? Here's a young man dying of leukemia, and this is the first time he has considered the possibility that God exists. A pat answer, such as "God is love," would turn him off. A broad philosophical answer was not what he was seeking either. However, the Holy Spirit has already answered, "Christ is the visible likeness of the invisible God (Col. 1:15, TEV)." Therefore, anything one could share about Jesus Christ's time on earth, his dealing with people, the things he said (all communicated in the Gospels), would communicate something of God's character.

What God brought to mind was the passage in Matthew 8:2-3 where a leper came to Jesus and said, "If you will, you can make me clean." And Jesus said, "I will." Then Jesus did something more. Besides healing the leper of his physical illness, he reached out and physically touched him. Do you know anything about lepers? In the time that Jesus was here on earth, if a leper even came near another person he had to call out "Unclean! Unclean!" They were never allowed to touch anyone and quite probably did not even touch each other. So here was a man who had not felt the touch of another human being for as long as he had had this disease, and Jesus reached out and touched him. God goes farther than what we think our needs to be. This man needed to "feel" part of the human race again, and Jesus knew and met this need.

Tom's response to this was, "Well, I'll think about it."

Tom got out of the hospital for about a month and a half. He went to a large university in the West to start his junior year and became so very sick that he had to come back. The first night I saw him, he said, "All I could think about was that I had to get back here and tell you what happened to me out there. You told me that God cares about each one of us even if we ignore him. I ended up with one of those 'Jesus freaks' for a roommate, and it hit me that God must care, to follow me all across country, and so I gave my life to Jesus Christ." Tom lived from November until March—all this time (except for six days home during Christmas) in the hospital. We had long talks about life and death. He talked a lot about wanting to live, but he never said much about a future. He took each day as it came.

His parents were supportive in the way they spent so much time with him, his mother being especially helpful because she was sensitive to his need to be quiet at times. She would sit in the room reading, but ready when he needed something.

After Tom died, I wrote his mother. Tom had been a friend, not just a patient, and I shared this in my letter. I told her how much it meant to all of us on the staff that she was so faithful and understanding with Tom. I didn't say anything about Tom's relationship with God because I didn't really know what he had told them. The following was her reply:

> I'm so glad that you wrote us, so that I can tell you how lucky we all three felt to know you, especially of course how blessed it was that you were there for Tom.
>
> I still can't at all understand how he could be so steady and patient under such mental and physical anguish, but I know that friendship like yours was central. Sometimes I'd wish that I had your experience at dealing with people, but then I'd realize that it wasn't expertise at all but innate warmth and friendship that made you so good for him.

When I received this letter, I knew that I had to tell her that it wasn't I but the Lord who gave Tom the grace to bear what he had gone through. I prayed for a long time regarding the way to share Tom's experience with Jesus Christ. I did not want to add to their already deep grief and knew the Lord would give the right words. The following was her reply to my second letter:

> Many thanks for writing. I am really glad that Tom had the consolation of religion—*anything* that could sustain him through so miserable a horror. Of course I could not possibly have helped him there, and I can only tell you again how grateful I am that he had you—above all, just you—as well as the benefits of your religion.
>
> And thanks, too, for the support and friendship you gave Fred and me. I see that you understand our inevitable sense of guilt and inadequacy, and, believe me, your reassurances have been a great help.

It has been a boon to know you, and if I ever have the need I will certainly call you.

Tom's mother did call me and asked me if she could come up to the hospital and have a cup of coffee with me. She needed to talk more about Tom's death and his faith in Jesus Christ. She also told me how, as a child, she was presented with a concept of God as one who only punishes. She wanted to continue to get together just to talk.

In summary, what does all this boil down to? What applications can be made on a broad spectrum as to meeting the needs of those who are dying and their families? Can only certain people be involved with patients in this way? Does this apply only to people who are dying, or can it be applied to anyone in crisis or to anyone just living in this hectic world today? What are the essential realities that must be faced?

Perhaps the first essential is the establishment of a relationship. We are told by Alvin Toffler in his book *Future Shock* that fewer and fewer meaningful relationships are being formed.[3] There is apparently a fear of involvement. I would rather go through the hurt that comes when someone like Tom dies than to carry the guilt of staying uninvolved.

A second reality to be considered is time. We in the nursing profession often say we do not have the time to get involved. A patient was admitted with smoke inhalation. Her apartment had caught fire. It was late in the evening and, though she had received medication to calm her down, she was very anxious. On rounds, I stopped in and asked her what she was most concerned about. She burst into tears and said that her dog had been burned to death in the fire. I told her that I understood what she must be feeling but, even more important, that the Lord was also hurting with her. Would she like me to pray with her? Her response was affirmative, and the prayer went something like this: "Father God, you know what deep sorrow Mrs. T. is feeling right now. You have given us animals to be a comfort to us, and it hurts so much when they are hurt or killed. Please surround Mrs. T with your deepest love, a very real sense of your presence. Please give her that peace which is beyond our understanding. In your Son's name, amen." A little later, I walked by this patient's room and she was sleeping peacefully. The time I spent with her was no more than five minutes. What this really says is that it is not the amount of time you spend with a patient but how you spend it. Sitting down in a patient's room for two minutes may be more profitable than standing in the doorway for fifteen.

A third essential needs to be put in the form of questions to each one of us: "How much do we really care?" "Do we dare to care about another person?" Paul hits us with this in 1 Corinthians 13. We can be the very best practitioners with tremendous skills, but if we don't care (have concern, love, charity), it is of little value. We are called to minister to whole people—physical, emotional, and spiritual beings. Hearing a nurse refer to "the gallbladder in Room Fifty-two" communicates to me a lack of care. We are free to choose to be mechanical in our work with patients, but I believe we need to confront ourselves with the reality that this is what we are doing.

Fourthly, if we are going to share the Lord with our patients (or even with those who are not patients), we have to know him ourselves. A seventy-three-year-old patient put it this way: "I've known all *about* Jesus all my life—now I know *him*." What is he really like? Does he really care about each one of us? Does he know us in our uniqueness as individuals, and does he want to communicate his love to us?

I was asked to take care of a "difficult" patient one day who had kicked the night nurse in the stomach. (Mrs. Q was with us while waiting for transfer to a mental institution. She was deaf and had severe liver disease—not caused by alcohol—and it was felt that she could no longer care for herself at home as she often became confused.) Upon entering Mrs. Q's room, I was told by the patient that she did not want a bath, she did not want her bed made, and she didn't want me. I left and went to a patient who liked me. But I could not get rid of the feeling that there was a purpose in my being assigned to Mrs. Q, so back in I went, having first said to the Lord, "You're my only reason for returning. Please somehow get through to this patient that you love her." This time I sat on the bed. Mrs. Q was reading a newspaper. She looked at me, sitting there on her bed, and began to talk. Her grandparents had come over from Ireland during the potato famine. Her mother had gone to work in a factory at age thirteen and was raped coming home one night—

hence Mrs. Q. (It had never crossed my mind before that someone sixty-five could be illegitimate.) Mrs. Q also had to go work in the factory at thirteen and was raped and got syphilis as a result, which led to her deafness. She then married and, when her husband was forty and their son five, her husband had a heart attack and fell off the scaffolding he was on and died. At this point tears began to run down my face. Mrs. Q seemed surprised and said, "You really care." Whatever words I might have said at this point would not have been heard, so I went out for a New Testament and showed her some passages which she read aloud. When she reached Matthew 11:28 and read, "Come to me, all of you who are tired from carrying your heavy loads, and I will give you rest (TEV)," she looked up and said, "This is beautiful. Who wrote it?" I took a piece of paper and wrote, "God wrote it because he wants you to know that he loves you."

Instead of going to an institution, Mrs. Q went home one week later, and to my knowledge she is still there. She believed God really did care and acted on it. She kept reading the New Testament as one who was very hungry, and it was beautiful to see. It was in her hand the day she left, and her parting comment to me was, as she held up her Bible, "This is going with me."

Finally, I'm left with a pressing burden, that everyone reading this chapter might dare to say to the One who has given us life —life in all its fullness—"God, use me. Use me with no strings attached. If I must look foolish, may I be a fool for Christ's sake and glory. Enable me to hear your voice and to be obedient to your directions, however strange they may seem. Make me sensitive to the needs of others, and cause me to trust that you will meet these needs because you care more about them than I ever could. In Jesus' name, amen."

4

Religion and Faith Together

BY DAVID JOHN ROCHE, R.N., A.D. SCI.

Religion and faith working together, in the eyes of the nurse, often take on the aspect of the "special" where healing is concerned. All too often nurses regard the phenomenon of cure as a matter concerning only the physician and his professional ministrations to his patients. But next to the physician, the nurse is most frequently with the patient. The more time we spend with patients, the more opportunities there are to observe their cures.

A student told me of a personal experience in which she and the patient involved shall remain anonymous.

"Mrs. A spent three months in a psychiatric hospital. During that time major changes in her life took place. Her social history shows that at the time of this admission she was married for the second time. She had one child from the first marriage and two stepchildren through her second marriage. She was well educated and held an executive position in a large civil service agency. She had spells of depression from the time of her first marriage, which ended in divorce.

"She recalls her admission to the hospital as a time when she had few controls left and was close to deep hysteria. She says at that time she had no desire to live or to die; she just didn't care any more one way or the other. She lost interest in her family, with the exception of her natural child, whom she says she never totally ignored in her despair. She stopped combing her hair, and it became increasingly difficult to get dressed for the day. Her doctors and nurses were competent, she believes, but initially she fought against letting anyone help her. Her withdrawal became so severe that at times she was mute, even when she wished to talk. She had to resign her job and let her relatives take care of her children.

"When she believed there was no hope for her, she began to experience a new perception. For some unexplainable reason she believed she was given a chance to rebuild her life through other patients in the hospital. She began to find people whom she could talk with and discovered there were others who were suffering as much or more than she was. One experience was with a mother who came back after being home on a pass from the institution. The woman was drunk and was going to take an overdose. When Mrs. A knocked the pills out of her hand, the woman began to sob. Mrs. A calmed her and told her of her two stepchildren; the mother of these stepchildren had taken her own life. Mrs. A further told this patient about the many problems the children had had as a result of their mother's death. That night, she says she thanked God for being able to think, for the first time in many weeks, of the pain of another being.

"In the following weeks and months Mrs. A became interested in several other patients in the division she was assigned to. She also began to work well with her psychiatrist. She joined a group on the 'outside' with the help of her doctor. This enabled her to help support other people who were fighting emotional illness. She used her own experience as a patient to empathize with others facing similar problems. She found that the more she did for others the better able she was to function. (She believes she was granted a very special gift, the ability to perceive the pain of another human being.) To her it meant both a fruitful life and a cure for her own emotional problems. She left her prestigious career and went to work in a hospital. She now says that she still has some tough periods but never has let them interfere with her functioning. She remembers that the staff who helped her never let her down, and she feels certain she could never let her patients down either.

"She is not sure what kind of power touched her, but she does feel it was a spiritual experience. Not particularly religious, she doesn't know what kind of labels to use. However she does remember that each time she became aware of another person's pain, she felt very grateful she could still feel and prayed she would find a way to reach out to the individual in question. It was something she didn't know was even a part of her—prior to that time—but she could feel it, and the more she used her feelings to perceive how others felt, the more alive she became. She also feels that free will was involved and can remember a particular day when she felt she could choose to remain an emotional cripple or use her awareness to fight her way out of it.

"It was as if she had been allowed to see how to use her experience constructively if she really wanted to relieve her own mental torment. She believed it had to have been something greater than herself that intervened in her life and gave her the strength to choose health over dependency."

Well-informed Christians and Jews should know that, within the structures of the various religious practices, formulas exist wherein the matter of faith is associated with healing.

I am taking the liberty, as a Roman Catholic and a registered nurse, to present a seldom-understood explanation of that religion's role in the matter of faith and healing. The spiritual implications cannot be separated from the medical situation. Traditionally, the services of the ordained priest and, more recently, those of the deacon have been requested in the case of the dying patient—that is, in situations where death seems imminent or has occurred usually within the time limit of two to three hours before the arrival of the priest/deacon (cases in which the physician has pronounced the patient "clinically deceased"). Further, what I am about to write must be understood from the viewpoint of one theology and is not intended to be a proselytization or a strict catechism.

Today Catholics do not limit their concern for the physically or mentally afflicted until death is nearly irreversible from the clinical standpoint. The recent writing of Vatican II greatly changed the attitude of the whole church in reference to its ministry to the dying. Formerly, our sacramentally based ritual for the dying—namely, Extreme Unction—was a ritual specifically reserved for the dying person. Tradition and misuse of this sacrament greatly restricted its use; the seriously terminal patient was often traumatically insulted.

What happened is that the hierarchy, through the study of both priestly and lay opinion, began to see the ritual as having great spiritual value not only for the terminally ill but also for the living. Perhaps the only common example that thousands know of is the practice of administering the "sacrament of the dying" (other than to the person in immediate danger of death) to hundreds of persons preparing for active combat in time of all-out war. This occurred many times in World War I and

World War II, not to mention Korea and Vietnam. (One exception will always stand out in my mind: At one time a group of Italians, preparing to do battle against a rival Italian contingent, approached Pope Pius X and beseeched him to bless their army before the fighting began. The venerable old man looked the commanding officer right in the eye and said, "I bless peace, not war!")

The original question posed was resolved in the last years of study concluded on the Documents of Vatican II—namely, that the Sacrament of the Dying, now changed to the Sacrament of the Living or the Sacrament of Eternal Life, should not be reserved only for the dying. Why, the fathers of Vatican II asked, should not this sacrament be permitted for the living as well? After all, who in all reality is exempt from sudden death? Do not people suffer cardiac arrest, do not pedestrians have accidents, do not people living in homes for the aged often "drop over," are there not mistakes in medication orders, is not food poisoning sometimes a reality? The traditional image of the priest ministering to the eighty-year-old victim of hypostatic pneumonia or the patient in the final stages of generalized arteriosclerotic heart and vascular disease no longer holds true.

The point to be brought out is the specific attitude of a formal religious theology and its trend toward a more "all-inclusive" concern for its members and the artifacts used in the Catholic ritual for the sick and dying. It is hoped, especially in a discussion of the latter, that the reader will more fully understand the specific methods used by Catholics in the matter of faith and healing.

Historically speaking, sacred scripture tells of many instances in which Jesus Christ cured individual people by the imposition of his hands or by his command to wash in specific bodies of water; there are also the remarkable events of Lazarus and ultimately his own resurrection from the dead. Believing Catholic Christians refer to these events of scripture as miracles or the miraculous intervention of God through the divine Person, Jesus Christ. We know, too, that Christ gave power, through the Holy Spirit, to selected followers, his apostles and disciples, to bring about miraculous "cures" and "events" in an age of men who greatly needed heavenly signs to demonstrate that the power of the Holy Spirit indeed was working through men.

What confuses so many Catholics and other Christians is the faith many people place in material objects which they feel are the true cause of a miraculous power. I should like to point out that objects, of themselves, to be used in the practice of faith and healing do not hold any superstitious power or magical quality. The answer lies mainly in the great and unquestioning gift of faith that the doer as well as the receiver of an act of "cure" or "restoration" to health has within his will.

So the old problem of statues, Holy Water, bread, salt, wine, oil, blessed candles, incense, and long formulas of prayer enter into the picture. If any basis for what is believed and practiced by Catholics exists, it must be the irrefutable combination of faith and prayers—faith in God and the ardent desire, through fervent prayer, that prayer is always answered, even if the answer does not immediately reflect a solution to the petition.

Most people have heard the old expression, "God works in strange ways." So true is this expression, that for most it is the bulwark of what maintains faith. As for unexplained phenomena where God was not "implored" for help, the average mind usually discounts the result to "consequence" or "good timing."

For the Catholic—and for most people, in general—the beauty of petition to God for help in time of need lies in the example given by prayerful persons who realize the power of God over disease. For if nothing else, at least human dependence is placed upon the "giver and receiver" of life, and this is fundamental for most, if not all, theologies, both Christian and Jewish. People, further, gather together to pray on the advice of Christ himself, who said, "Where two or three are gathered in my name, I too am in their midst."

Have I seen what appears to have been a participation of the forces of God intervene in the art, spirit, skill, and science of medicine? I believe so. And I have reason to suspect that many physicians, perhaps alone, have gotten down on their knees either to thank God for that "mysterious" intervention or maybe to ask of God, "How?"

The very fact that many Catholic physicians, after viewing all the circumstances in cases of terminal cancer, for example, pronounce the prognosis as moribund, but still do not discontinue palliative treatment, shows their probable belief that a small margin of time for a reversal of the disease process does exist, even though their own knowledge has been exhausted. It is at this point, I suppose, that physicians, nurses, family, and probably the patients themselves often turn covertly to God and whatever his will might be. If not, cases of enthusiastic hope would reverse to cases of euthanasia, possibly far more than exist, according to the records.

As for people traveling to parts of the world where, scientifically and medically, miracles seem to have occurred—and I am speaking of Lourdes, France; Fatima, Portugal; Saint Anne de Beaupré, Quebec, Canada; the Shrine of Saint Mary of Guadalupe, Mexico, D.F.—my only remark is that most people who undertake such pilgrimages seem to have an extraordinary gift of faith. Furthermore, that the documented record of "cures" or "miracles" usually coincides with people who so strongly believe in miracles seems to show the strong relationship between faith and the background of such "faithhealing" centers.

A personal experience of my own involves a now deceased religious lay brother of the Third Order of Saint Francis, of which I was also a member at one time, an account simple but incredible when one examines the overall picture of one man's faith over the power of Satan.

For years this elderly, devout widower, admitted to a religious order of men dedicated to the care of the infirm, aged, and chronically afflicted, worked humbly, without any professional credentials, as a night orderly in a division of aged male patients. The old men involved were considered ambulatory in that they could rise from their beds to use bathroom facilities, get into wheelchairs, or walk with canes or walkaids. The bulk of nursing services necessary in this area of the nursing home included supervising medications, changing beds, general cleaning, and extraordinary measures as needed. Obviously the services required of the lay brother were minimal from 11:00 P.M. to 7:00 A.M.

Nightly, however, up and down the hall he would go, shaking drops of Holy Water into each patient's doorway, offering a muted petition of benevolence and protection from God for the old men sleeping inside. He did this for all the years he worked in the capacity of a lay brother, even when nearing the end of his own life. He believed ardently—steadfastly—in the invisible power of the blessed substance of the Holy Water and, even more, in the protection he felt it afforded those with whom it came in contact. You can well believe that the younger religious workers, as they learned of his practice, wondered at his activity and suppressed their own skepticism. After all, maybe there was something to it. Others who had seen him doing this "sprinkling" approached the old brother and asked him about it. "Brothers," he said, "every night I take this bottle of Holy Water and sprinkle it up and down the floor in each patient's room. Do you know, after I have finished, there isn't one sound or hint of restlessness in the whole place? I have been doing this for thirteen years, and I believe that the Devil can't get into any of those rooms once I have sprinkled it with Holy Water. There's something wonderful about the Holy Water. It seems to help the old men sleep more quietly, and I don't have to worry about any of them going to hell if they should die." Well, that is that. He persisted in this practice, and one had to admire his conviction that Holy Water held the key to the personal security of each patient in that place throughout each and every night. (That same individual, by the way, had lived a most remarkable life and was full of unusual stories where his own health and life were concerned.)

Briefly, as a last example of faith and healing, I would like to turn to a personal experience in which I was involved, the case of a dying priest who fought a death agony the likes of which I had never seen or heard of before.

The old priest, so aged and so advanced in his generalized arteriosclerotic disease process, could barely walk without staggering, not only because of his advanced state of debility but also because of the impairment of his equilibrium.

In his prime he had been known from Missouri to Texas, in France, and in other places where he had been assigned as a teacher of theology and a confessor. Members of his religious society testified that literally hundreds of people would come to him to have their confessions heard. He held a degree of Doctor of Theology, spoke French fluently, and was one of the most kindly and pious gentlemen I had ever come to know. Sad it was, however, that my first meeting with him occurred shortly after his admission to a "locked" division of a professional nursing home. At the time of his admission, his mind was so grossly incapacitated by the multiple problems of advanced generalized arteriosclerosis that for the most part the staff regarded him as impossibly, incurably senile. Existing in a world of his own, he clung tenaciously to the regimen he had so scrupulously followed as an active priest and teacher, arranging with people to hear confessions, have benediction, lecture in class, and give counsel to "problem" boys in the "school" he believed himself to be a part of. Nobody was able to bridge the gap between his formerly active apostolate and his present life of inactivity on a ward for the seriously (though not dangerously) mentally defective. He was so disoriented as to time and place that he even forgot to dress. Often he would be seen wearing only a soutane without any undergarments. He would carefully slip into the chapel, remove the Mass Book, and proceed to have Mass in his own room. His priestly powers had been dispensed to protect penitents from his possible breaking of the seal of what is said confidentially in confession and because he was no longer able to concentrate on the formula of the Mass ritual. Life for him was frustrating, lived, as it were, between reality and the past, with a few brief episodes of clear contacts with reality and the unexplainable knowledge that for all general purposes he had become a prisoner with so many "of our very sick brothers," as he referred to the rest of the patients around him.

His terminal illness lasted about ten days, a time in which many of his former associates visited him. He knew none of them, even forgetting our purpose for being with him. On the next-to-last day of his illness, he was restrained in bed because he insisted upon getting to Mass, hearing confessions, and having Benediction for the community before they were to retire. Throughout his whole death agony, he clung to a rosary and his breviary with a physical strength beyond description. In his garbled and infrequent conversation, he alternately prayed and cursed the "devil" whom he felt to be lurking at his bedside, eager to clutch his soul and carry it off to hell. As religious and nurses, we attended him without interruption from shift to shift. His major religious superior came to the bedside to pray in the name of his society for his spiritual reward and comfort in his death agony. The patient never recognized anyone. During our ministrations, we struggled with him to keep his arm restrained so that the intravenous infusion would not come apart.

He would alternate between fits of yelling, praying, and weeping and deathlike comatose periods.

He died, alone with a nursing brother, in the dead of night after a hectic day of the same kind of activity. Of special note were the times that the chaplain would come to give this priest-patient Holy Communion. At the reception of the Eucharist, all former anxiety and fear, all hysteria and yelling would subside, and a calm and quiet atmosphere would fill the whole room. This would last for fifteen to thirty minutes. The nursing staff was able to wash his body, check the I.V., and even carry on some limited rational conversation with the otherwise "violent" patient.

This demonstration of faith and religious practice with this exceptional patient leads up to a specific matter for discussion that must, I feel, be included in any study of faith and healing. For the Catholic Church has many practices that are vastly different from the rituals of other faiths.

I have dealt mainly with what the Catholic Church does in regard to the dying patient. I am sure that interested readers would have no difficulty in locating accounts of miraculous cures of people in such places as Lourdes and Fatima by asking any Catholic priest for information.

Most practices of faith and healing within the formal structure of the Catholic Church, which obviously I am most familiar with, deal with sacramentals. This term is widely used, misunderstood, and unexplained, for the most part, where Catholics and non-Catholics are concerned. Therefore, I feel it necessary to include in this chapter a brief explanation of what sacramentals are and why they play so important a part in the religious ritual of Catholics, especially in matters of sickness, suffering, and death.

Simply defined, a sacramental refers to an artifact used in a liturgical function, formal or informal (involving a priest or a layman). Sacramentals include a wide range of simple items used by the minister (priest) of the rite, in which their significance represents an outward sign or symbol of some more profound and intangible religious belief.

Included among the more common sacramentals are water, salt, oil, candles, incense, wine, and bread. These "artifacts" of liturgical worship are most commonly associated with Roman

Catholic liturgical functions. Throughout history these material symbols have accrued great notoriety as to their meaningfulness and/or pure "superstition." Obviously even the most educated of men have questioned the value of a pinch of salt placed on a baby's tongue during the Rite of Baptism. Skeptics argue the validity of material symbolism to the point of real wonder. Yet the Roman Catholic Church persists in the use of such objects. There is a great lesson which can be learned from a more open-minded understanding of the practices involved in the sacred rites of any religious faith.

What has happened, however, is that certain individuals of the faithful (worshiping) body of the church, because of some unusual experience involving the use of sacramentals, have misconstrued the value and meaning of a sacramental and, as such, have attributed undue and wrongful value to the artifact in question. The old notion, so firmly implanted even in the minds of the most sincere and devout individuals, stands the weathered test of argument each time, and consequently the observer usually goes away greatly miseducated and even more distracted and distrustful of the whole business. The simple remedy is to attempt to inform the knowledgeable public as to the true meaning and reason for having a system of sacramental liturgics within such a complex structure as the Catholic faith. The rest is up to the reader, who must ultimately choose whether to accept or reject the explanation.

Most things, sacramentals included, can only receive credit where credit is due. As a matter of fact, the church probably has more difficulty in holding down her own members and their misconstrued ideas about sacramentals than any other group of persons. As mentioned earlier, experience with sacramentals that appear to have magical or superior powers easily can lead the observer and/or the beneficiary into believing that Holy Water possesses of itself such a tremendous effect as to rout every devil from his lair within fifty miles. Nonetheless, good, upright, and reverent Catholics are still living who firmly believe in the extraordinary power of such a thing as Holy Water and the effects it will have when used to eliminate evil situations. Such individuals even go to the extent of having a small bottle of the stuff at their beck and call, especially at night, at the bedside, so that if any unusual event should occur, even the sense of impending danger or death itself, a few shakes of the bottle will solve a lifetime of miserable worry and living, leaving the victim free to gain entry into the heavenly kingdom for all eternity. This is not intended to be a disrespectful or facetious remark. I must refer you to my earlier example of the religious lay brother and his unquestioning faith in the effects of Holy Water.

I believe that Holy Water and any of the other sacramentals I have cited, used in personal or private devotion, are strictly symbols representative of theological precepts involved in the liturgical activity of the specific rite. As such, they have frequently been blessed before or are so blessed during the special liturgical function in which they will be involved. In every case, the name and supreme authority of God is invoked in the prelude to the blessing, in such a way, by the officiating minister—who can be a priest, bishop, or pope—so that all who witness the blessing and subsequent use of the sacramental can understand the significance of the blessed items.

Most often, if not always, within the rite of blessing, recognition of the material substance and its intended use is acknowledged, thanking the Creator of such substance for his generous gift of same, and imploring his blessing on it so that it may be used only for the highest good so that mankind will see the example of how things ought to be used rather than abused.

The foregoing is the greatest lesson learned from the proper use of sacramentals and, as such, fairly demands the respect of the believing faithful when these artifacts are used. An interesting account of the reasons for the limited number of items chosen for use as sacramentals can be found in most encyclopedias, not to mention the vast resources on sacramentals in most Catholic college and university libraries. The curious reader should no more feel ashamed to inquire of these things than feel fearful of investigating the whole matter of faith and healing.

One may logically ask, just why is the water blessed? After having been blessed, the water is credited with the symbolism of washing, just as it has been used throughout history in almost every social system known to man. Specifically, in the Rite of Baptism, water is the universal "solvent" used by most faiths that employ water as the vehicle of absolution or cleansing of sin according to the ancient Christian rite. One only needs to refer to sacred scripture and the account of John the Baptist and the baptism of Christ to see the importance of running water as the focal point of the rite. (The water, in that case, was not formally blessed, but tradition and reverence for the Son of God allow us to believe that the contact the water made with the person of Christ gave it added significance and symbolism.)

One finds himself really wondering why water, and not some other substance, was used for baptism. The prophets foretold that water would be used. As part of the Divine Plan of God for the salvific way for all men, water figured greatly in God's designs. Read Genesis. How profound is the account of the creation of the great oceans and seas! How formidable that water was one of the first things created, and how necessary it is for the very life and existence of all men! As mentioned earlier, water is the universal solvent. Isn't it beautiful that such a plentiful substance as water has been made available for men and is so easily gotten and widely available for use in combating the many chemical problems man has to deal with? Has it not been said that soap and water are two of the least expensive things around? In comparing the cleansing effects of water, maybe it is easier for people to see why so many faiths have incorporated water into their liturgies.

In conclusion, I would be most agreeable that the phenomena of faith and healing go hand in hand. Truly, most physicians and nurses at some time or other base much of their covert feelings toward a kind of believing pact with the Creator that the efforts of both contribute to whatever the outcome might be wherein the patient is concerned.

Time has shown the interest of men in the hereafter, from the discoveries made in ancient tombs where religious artifacts were seen side by side with the remains of the deceased; from accounts of rudimentary practices of medicine by Greeks who implored their gods for intervention in sickness; from the accounts of the Salem witch trials in which ministers battled with the "occult" forces of satanic characters for mastery over disease and death; and even in our own day, as we witness the minister, rabbi, or priest giving spiritual care to the dying alongside the highway, in the operating room, or at the hospital bedside.

One question will probably haunt us until the end of time: Will death ever be overcome through the direct intervention of man without the apparent intervention of him whom we call God? Perhaps man's demonstration for the mysterious things in life is what holds him to the mysteries of faith. For in faith there are many things that people do not understand. We merely accept such phenomena on the basis of faith.

5
A Christian Attitude – Does It Make a Difference?

BY DORIS V. DOUDS, R.N.

Long before Jesus' time, ancient pagan "wonder workers" performed miracles of a nature similar to Jesus' healings. In reading the Gospels and the accounts of the miracles, one is met head on with Jesus' insistence that "by faith" we are made whole—that is, body and soul, mind and spirit, can be put into harmony only by total belief in the harmonizing agent, whether it be faith in God or in a human intermediary.

The area of psychosomatics is not new; even Hippocrates took into consideration the sick person's spiritual needs as well as his bodily ills.

Those of us in medicine and related services have increasingly become aware of this relationship. It is clear that our thoughts often become manifested in somatic responses, for good or ill. There is ample evidence of this. Emotions (hate, greed, resentment, lust, envy, self-adulation) often are basic ingredients for the development of ulcers, cardiac conditions, upper respiratory diseases, alcoholism, drug addiction, or proneness to accidents. This fact has been proven.

In the same manner, primary physical illness works to distort and sometimes destroy the working of the mind, and therefore affects the core of our being—the soul, or spirit—and so the cycle begins.

I am reminded of Jesus' question to the man who had lain beside the pool for many years: "Do you really want to be well?" Jesus sensed that the man was self-pitying, making excuses and evading, and was unwilling to face the responsibilities of living a normal life, should he be returned to health.

Physicians and nurses are aware that there are many in hospital beds who could be well if they really wanted to be. It seems to be true that if one is not willing, he cannot be cured.

In recent years there has been a great surge toward psychological and spiritual counseling as a regular service in hospitals. This past year when I was facing surgery, my physician sent me to talk with the staff psychiatrist. His words were, "I want to know your attitude toward sickness, surgery, handicap. I need to know more in depth how you feel about life." In this discussion, the psychiatrist drew out my whole confession of faith and trust and belief. On hearing this, he smiled and said, "You will do well; and I want you to know that those whose religion is at the heart of life fare much better than those who have little or no faith." Years ago the noted psychiatrist Karl Menninger said, "I have never treated successfully a patient with no faith or hope."

In thinking about this, my mind dwells on the word "attitude." Over many years as a Christian nurse it has been apparent to me that committed Christians who continually and daily draw strength from their faith face physical and mental crises, and even death, with greater assurance and peace of mind. Believing in the ultimate power of God to do all things, and trusting in him to bring about that harmony of body and spirit, many Christians have an "attitude" toward wholeness that aids in healing. The changing, through faith, of an attitude of fear and distrust to one of hope and trust is to me the great miracle.

One doctor told me that in thirty-six years' practice he had learned that only God heals, and that healing depends largely on the patient's inner harmony with himself and God. "There is a real connection," he said, "between the physical and the spiritual." This connection produces an attitude which comes only in that special relationship between man and the divine.

Our attitudes are affected by those around us, as we affect them. Each of us can cite some person who has greatly influenced our attitudes: a parent, friend, teacher, minister, or doctor. Then, too, there are ideas coming to us continually through history, past or present, which influence us. Most important of all is the influence of a personal experience of Christ.

My convictions as related to the changing of attitude are based on my study of Jesus' method of healing.

First, Jesus listened. He was extraordinarily sensitive to the fears and needs, both physical and spiritual, of others. Nothing shocked him. He heard not so much what was said but the way in which it was said. He responded to a tone of voice, an anxious expression, a body posture, a reaching and trembling hand, the falling of a tear. For that moment Jesus gave his attention fully to that person. He himself spoke little. In Proverbs 12:25 we read: "Anxiety in a man's heart weighs him down, but a good word makes him glad." Again, in the book of Job is a request: Keep silent toward me, that I may speak, and *something will pass away from me.* Today, as Jesus did, psychologists, psychiatrists, men of God also recognize the importance and validity of listening.

Second, Jesus showed *compassion.* One can imagine his hand resting on the head or shoulder of the seeker, or his warm steady gaze into pleading eyes, offering quietness and calmness.

Third, Jesus offered *reassurance.* By expressing his faith in those who came to him, he bolstered each one's faith in himself. Often Jesus spoke words like the following from Luke 8:48: "Your faith has saved you" (made you whole, in harmony). One can imagine hope springing up to take the place of fear, trust thrusting upward and outward to him and his perfect faith, and mental and spiritual recharging in response to his power.

Fourth, having roused them out of a state of apathy and hopelessness, Jesus performed a simple physical act, such as laying his hands on their heads or, as in the case of one blind man, putting spittle mixed with dirt on the man's eyes. There are many such examples in the stories of healing, for this was an acceptable and expected and understood method among healers in that period.

Following the act on the part of Jesus, the petitioner was required to respond himself—that is, to take his responsibility in a specific way. Said Jesus, "Go, show yourself to the priests," "Go, wash yourself," "Go, and be reconciled," "Go, and tell," "Return to your home," "Stretch out your hand."

This requirement was and is basic, was and is a part of the way toward a change in attitude.

This is also the way of confession and penance in the Catholic Church, of ministerial counseling and involvement of the person in witness and service in the Protestant Church, of psychiatric counseling and therapy, of medical counseling and treatment. One must *do* something, in response, for change and healing to take place.

Among the early Christians were many who were able to transform and heal, but not all. At one time even Jesus failed, because of his inability to reach the people whose faith in him was too little to call out response.

Later the disciples, lacking full faith, were unable to help or to heal. Once their attitude was changed, miracles of healing occurred.

It seems, then, that confidence must be mutual if results are to be obtained. Healer—either medical, psychological, or spiritual—and patient must cooperate.

Only twice in my career, out of literally thousands of cases, have I seen what is termed "faith healing," neither one being instantaneous but, to my mind, the result of belief in the power of God to heal. One patient was a forty-year-old woman with nine living children. She was brought in hemorrhaging. Pathological examination of tissue revealed cancer. When the patient was told that surgery was essential, she refused. "I'm a devout Catholic," she calmly remarked. "Call the priest." In the presence of her family, the doctor, and myself, the patient expressed her faith, was given communion, and a circle of joined hands was formed. The priest anointed her head, and we all prayed silently. Within twenty-four hours, the bleeding had stopped. The prayer circle was repeated several times during the following week, and masses were offered in her name. She never had surgery, and though she was in the hospital for weeks undergoing local applications of (of all things) raw tungsten oil, the ultimate result was a complete cure—which I witnessed. I am convinced that without that faith and the trust and belief which she, her family, her friends, and her church had, this woman would have died. Her attitude, being wholeness and harmony within herself and with God, brought about a true miracle—in time.

Another woman (who was a friend of mine), a warm, outgoing person, gave birth to an infant daughter who was not expected to live through the night. A prayer vigil was kept for the mother and child by a group of her friends. The child did live, but the outcome was indeed a miracle of a different sort of healing. Discovering that the infant was severely brain damaged, the mother at first had problems with her faith, until when the child was two years old she offered her to an experimental drug program being carried on in Bethesda, Maryland. Through her child, a great contribution was made to medical science and to future generations. Since then my friend has told me many times that the real miracle was a spiritual one. The little girl was not physically healed, but the mother was spiritually healed by her change of attitude. She is now helping hundreds of others in her work with and for retarded children. "My gift child," she said, "has brought us much joy, and we are daily thankful for her."

I have been told the following, which again illustrates the role of the Christian's attitude toward illness and the necessity of the patient to act on his belief.

A famous baseball player, a member of the Church of Latter-Day Saints, was badly injured in a game. On being told that he would probably never swing a bat again, he sank into apathy and self-pity. His wife asked the elders of the church to come and pray for healing. They anointed his head with oil as prescribed in the Bible. They laid their hands on his head, asking for God's healing in the name of Jesus Christ. Afterward, though pain still existed, his attitude changed toward wholeness. He recognized his responsibility to his own side of prayer—to act.

The statement he made is clear evidence of his understanding: "Pray as if everything depended on God; work as if everything depended on you." He knew that God would heal him if he handled his own responsibility. Praying hard, working hard, doing long and painful exercises did bring full healing, and he returned to the game he never thought to play again—in time.

On the other hand, witnessing healing services, and reading of instantaneous healing, always disturbs me. I believe, and yet I doubt. In a highly dramatic atmosphere, accompanied by tremendous staging, publicizing, and in the presence of an excitable personality, vulnerable and emotionally charged ill people may be harmed by a delusion of healing that does not last beyond the exit door. I suspect that many have been disappointed afterward, when they had to come down off the mountaintop into the pain and suffering of daily living without the continuing stimulation of the "healing scene."

The possibility always exists, however, for that one-to-one exchange with exhortations and loud amens in the background to result in a change of attitude which may alter the course of a life in the direction of a clearer, closer, fuller faith, a new harmony between body and soul—and healing.

This brings me to the "Jesus people." I believe that God has again acted in history, and that the spirit of Christ is again moving and living among thousands of young people. If their approach to conversion, fundamental beliefs, the Bible, and Jesus offends the prim and proper and unemotional institutional church, then I believe we stiff-backed churchgoers should take a closer look at our own beliefs and actions. We should thank God for this developing change in attitude. Instead of condemning this resurgence of faith from nonfaith, this renewal of the fundamental beliefs and faith from the agnostic and atheist view, we should be humble.

The fact that youth is responding, however immaturely and, in some cases, questionably, should excite us to action. Instead of distorting their aims, which fundamentally call for healing in body, mind, and spirit through an experience with Jesus Christ, we should more openly and strongly declare our mutual faith. God truly moves in mysterious and wondrous ways to draw us unto himself. His is the only power to unite, to create harmony, to change the mind from a shattered, splintered, separated-from-God one to a mind that is inseparable from the spirit and therefore inseparable from the body.

Here again my conviction is based on Jesus' words—"Be one with me, as I am one with the Father." "To them who love God, all things are possible." Oneness, wholeness of body and spirit, the Christian attitude toward *totality*, expressed in each individual through belief, acceptance, obedience, and action, is dependent on the original premise that a Christian belief, and trust in God and the life and teachings of Jesus Christ, has an immeasurable effect. In this confession of faith lies unlimited possibilities for mental health, physical health, and spiritual health.

One word must be acknowledged as basic, the word love. Without love, we are nothing. Without love, infants wither and die. I can bear testimony to this. In the last ten years our family has loved and nurtured twenty-one unwanted children, some with physical illnesses or handicaps. Psychologists, doctors, social workers, nurses have all maintained that a child who is not loved, cuddled, held, given a sense of being wanted, truly does wither, withdraw, and die, spiritually and mentally, and sometimes physically.

Adults are no different. The Gospels stress love. "Love me ... love one another ... love God ... love your neighbor as yourself." Without love one perishes.

If one is going to live, and live creatively and wholly, one must learn to love in the Christian sense.

Young people today say that religious emphasis and experience is deepened as they share, touch, communicate. The emphasis is on fellowship with Christian love and caring. This love is a love that expresses deep agape feeling for others. It is a love not easily transmitted by words but by actions.

The Gospels indicate that a wholesome, loving respect for oneself means that one can truly love another. If we do respect and love ourselves as children of God, we can in the same way love and respect another as a child of God.

With, therefore, total love of God and Jesus Christ, and oneself—that is, the harmony of body, mind, and spirit (as Jesus taught and made central to his teachings)—a Christian approaches illness and handicap with the assurance that God gave that we might have. What happens to the Christian who alters his attitude toward ill health and strengthens his belief in the power of God to heal? If one is saying, "It can't happen to me," then I say, "How do you know it won't happen to you? How do you know great things won't happen?" The answer is, a different self-image, through Jesus Christ, and belief and therefore change in life attitude to living fully and completely in and out of physical and mental illness.

Never let us minimize the power of Jesus Christ to transform and change our attitude of self-centeredness and tendency toward ill health to an attitude of wholeness, health, selflessness, love of others, and the change of attitude through faith in God, in Christ, and in our brothers.

In conclusion, the Christian's attitude does make a vital difference in his behavior and approach to the problems of ill health, mental illness, and spiritual ills.

The psychosomatic school of practitioners and thinkers should be increased as fast as possible.

Doctors must recognize the existence of the human soul and, on that principle, act psychosomatically.

There is need for increasing cooperation between the clergy and the medical profession, nurses and doctors alike.

The patterns of health are woven not only out of the somatic but out of thought, faith, friendship, joy, loyalty, and sacrifice.

Wholeness—the harmony of body, soul, and mind—is the committed Christian's answer. The Christian attitude, that of total belief, trust, obedience, and most of all love, can and does produce healing and oneness with him who came to establish the kingdom of God in the hearts and minds of mankind then and now.

6
Faith, Thought, Feeling, and Healing

BY FLORENCE R. DURKEE, R.N., M.A.

Faith is the major factor in healing illness. The patient may have a religious faith in God that he will be healed, or he may be a confirmed atheist, agnostic, or infidel, but faith in being healed he must have.

Webster defines faith as "confidence or trust in a person or thing; belief which is not based on proof; belief in the doctrines and teachings of religion." From this it will be seen that faith per se is any belief, religious or otherwise, that an individual may hold. So the role of faith in healing should not be identified as being of a purely religious nature. It must rather be understood that by faith is meant a belief or trust that somehow healing will occur.

In the instances of so-called "faith healing" of a religious nature, the belief of the patient has been placed in God as an all-powerful and benevolent Creator who has heard and granted the supplication by the patient, his family, and friends to restore him to wholeness of body and mind. When the atheist or agnostic is healed, as many are, it is because he has believed he could be healed; he has had faith in his doctor or in the treatment prescribed to heal him or in the ability of his own body to heal itself.

An examination of each of these approaches to healing reveals a common denominator: there is belief or faith in healing that is positive and constructive. A still closer examination of the belief in healing raises the question of how this faith is expressed in us. Aside from the dictionary definition, what really is faith and how does it work?

Surprising as it may seem to many, faith or belief is simply one's thought process. It is impossible to think or feel anything at all without simultaneously setting faith into action. This is because of the behavior of the central nervous system in our bodies. Every waking second of our lives, thought processes go on inside us that for the most part are not appreciated or understood for the dynamic action of faith. Consequently we neither understand nor appreciate the effects which our own thoughts produce in our lives. We are sad or happy, sick or well, and never suspect our own thinking habits to be the cause.

The role of faith, then, in any individual is identical with the role of thought. If the physiology of our central nervous system and the importance of the reaction between it and the powerful endocrine gland had always been understood, there could never have been any doubt as to the cause of health or the lack of it in our lives.

It is the functioning of these two dynamic physical mechanisms in our bodies that clearly demonstrates the involvement of the patient's own thought and feeling with his healing or lack of it. Simultaneous with the thought flashed into the brain, feeling occurs. This is simply because the thought through the stimulus-response reaction of the body's five sensors has alerted the powerful endocrine gland system to react with appropriate secretions to bring about the feeling to match the thought. "Feeling" is produced basically by a chemical reaction between hormones (secretions) of the endocrines and the nervous system.

There are two fundamental responses to the hormone adrenalin (which is produced by glands situated atop each kidney): fight or flight. What hormones are released when we feel happy, secure, filled with love, and so on? Science has not yet provided us with the answers to this question. But it is safe to predict that one day, and possibly very soon, this will also be known.

In the case of the sick individual, does a flight reaction mean surrender to the malady? And does a fight reaction mean that faith for healing is being generated? While it cannot yet be scientifically proven that such is the case, we do know that blood pressure rises, breathing is more rapid, and the heart pounds when we are angry. Adrenalin is responsible for these feelings, as can be demonstrated by injecting adrenalin into the body.

What of the role of thought and feeling in the action of other endocrine secretions in the body? What secretions do they release and what do they do once they are in the bloodstream?

How do they react with adrenalin—if they do? It is known that secretions of both the pituitary and thyroid glands do indeed react with the secretions of the adrenal gland. Many theories exist as to the effects of such interaction, and there are some scientifically established facts about them, but no proof exists that such interaction is either detrimental or constructive in the healing of a disease that is related to the thoughts and feelings of the patient.

Doctors have known since Hippocrates and possibly even before that the body heals itself automatically if allowed to do so. Dr. Alexis Carrel[1] years ago demonstrated that living cells do not die if kept in a state of homeostasis. He kept a chicken heart alive for twenty-seven years in a balanced culture medium in a controlled atmosphere. The chicken heart, of course, could not feel or think. Man does both, and his thoughts and feelings must be considered as a powerful force for or against healing.

Until research and instruments are available to analyze the thoughts and feelings of a significant number of patients, both in cases of healing and of death, the foregoing must remain a hypothesis only. Yet physiologists have clearly proved the existence of the stimulus-response mechanism of the body, as well as the physiological effect of at least one powerful hormone, adrenalin.

The case of one woman who has been healed is given here, complete with her thoughts and feelings for the reader to ponder and draw his own conclusions.

Mrs. John Hart of Clinton, Iowa, went to her doctor for a general unwell feeling. Her abdomen seemed unusually large, and she was tired most of the time. After a week of tests in the hospital, her doctor informed her she must have surgery. Her story follows in her own words.

"I must tell of my spiritual communion with God on that Saturday before surgery the following Monday. At 10:30 P.M. three close friends prayed with me on my behalf and sent out thoughts of healing for me. I lay completely relaxed, visualizing myself lying in God's big white hand and putting all my trust in him. I fell asleep immediately afterward, feeling very much comforted.

"Following the surgery the surgeons would not look at my husband as they said, 'Cancer—three years at the most.' It was a day or two later before they told me they had opened me up and had sewed me back together again with nothing being removed. A liver biopsy had been done; that was all.

"For a day or two it was a lonely, desolate battle with my thoughts. I desired more than anything to see my little granddaughter grow up. The prospect now seemed to deprive me of that. As I think back, it was easy to give up this world's goods and pleasures, but I found it hard to relinquish the idea of seeing my granddaughter grow up.

"I decided to fight. I had prayers to say, and every hour on the hour I prayed to a particular saint, plus saying many rosaries. And all the while I was knowing and feeling a closeness with God, my master.

"It was amazing to my doctors how quickly I was able to care for myself. To their great surprise I ate everything on my food trays. They even accused my husband of eating my food. Their exploratory surgery had convinced them that I would be unable to eat anything at all.

"Then the report came from the laboratory on the specimen taken during the surgery: 'Cirrhosis of the liver.' I immediately began visualizing a perfect liver of normal size. Sometimes I talked to my liver, thanking it for sustaining me!

"At first I had to eat a lot of hard candy my doctor ordered, but now I rarely feel the need for candy as a source of energy. I *know* my energy comes from God and the very air I breathe. Within that first year I painted three sides of our house and helped my husband build a house for our daughter and her family. I carried lumber, nailed, and climbed ladders just like he did. I also carried on my usual work at home and my social life.

"Now I eat whatever I want. I sleep well. I have a zest for living, and I know that my God, the Supreme Being, is always with me. Daily I live with the rhythm of the universe and I meditate."

Thirteen references are made in the foregoing to thought and prayer, knowing and trusting, and faith in God to heal. All of these are most positive and optimistic. In her interview, Mrs. Hart made two emphatic statements about the whole situation. She said, "I just never doubted that I would recover," and "I decided to fight." Her motivation was an important factor in her return to health; she deeply desired to see her little granddaughter grow to maturity. There must always be a strong motive to be healed.

Since Mrs. Hart is a deeply religious woman, her faith, she states, was totally that she was in God's hands and would recover. Her doctor's behavior was not that which would have given her any faith in his ability to heal her. First the diagnosis had been wrong and the time span for her to live had been three years. That period is now up and she is in good health today. If cirrhosis still exists, she has no symptoms of it.

While cirrhosis is not as often identified with death as cancer it is none the less a terminal condition and not one which modern medicine has been able to reverse. Its progress toward termination of life may be slow or fast, depending upon the individual.

"Looking back on it," Mrs. Hart states, "the thing that amazes me is that I *never* gave up. I just *knew* I was going to recover." Her "knowing" was a deep, unshakable faith in God as her healer. Such is the faith that moves mountains. It is easier for the one with such faith to be healed, for God is the all-powerful Supreme Being. It is easy to trust such strength and power. But there are those hardy souls whose belief in their bodies to heal themselves is such that they also recover from critical illness. And if they cannot trust the body, they place their faith in their doctor or his medicines to heal them in an equally firm way and without any association with God.

Perhaps a word should be said here about prayer. Is it also a thought process? It is indeed identical to any other thought. The only difference between thought and prayer is that prayer is usually addressed to God and in a devotional attitude. But the physiological process is exactly the same as though we were talking to or about our next-door neighbor. There is no difference. Whether or not our thoughts are addressed to God, he hears them all: angry, resentful, complaining, worrying, or pleading for help and healing. They are all answered in exactly the way we direct them to him or to our neighbor, because it is our own faith in the situation which brings results. God must act through us. He cannot wave a magic wand and change all the laws of thought to please each whim we have.

Does this make man his own supreme power? Hardly. Let it not be forgotten that we did not create man, we merely recreate him in God's image. We did not endow man with his mighty mind, we merely use (or misuse) it. God is the author of our being whether or not we believe it. And God is the author of the faculty of thought. Through it we are co-creators with him him for every condition of our lives.

When the atheist uses his thought to believe in a return to full health from a diseased condition he is using a God-given faculty, and his belief in the existence of God is in no way important. Whether or not we consider him to exist, he does. And he installed in us a central nervous system which works cooperatively with an endocrine gland system to give orders to every cell in our bodies to obey our thoughts and feelings.

None of the foregoing is meant to say that one single thought, such as "Now I'm healed of this paralyzing condition," is going to be instantly effective or even effective at all. Everything in this universe of ours is governed by law and order and right conditions. That goes for healing too. There are laws which govern healing of any kind and there are conditions that must be met before healing can occur. That healing does sometimes occur instantly through prayer for the sick individual has made us look at such occurrences as something mysterious and miraculous.

And what is a miracle? Only the occurrence of an event for which there seems no existing law or explanation. Actually, however, that which seems to be a miracle is the result of the working out of laws of which we are still unaware. But they exist, and when we knowingly or unknowingly set them into action, something happens. Basic to the working of laws of healing is the law of faith being set into operation through deep desire.

There must be positive conviction that healing is to be the result of thought action. It is possible but very difficult for the sick individual to discipline his thoughts to concentrate on faith in wholeness of being when pain and weakness are the reality. For this reason, many persons who are ill need the assistance of others to bring about their recovery. Of course, prayer is an integral part of such assistance. But prayer for the healing of another must be accompanied by thoughts of faith and feelings of confidence in the well-being of the one prayed for.

When we believe sick persons are to be healed by our prayers, we cannot continue to see them lying in a bed in the hospital or at home, talk about their pain, or feel sorry for them and their family. Our prayer of supplication for their healing will be totally negated by such thoughts. That kind of thinking is not faith in healing at all. The only faith in operation under those circumstances is faith in their continued illness.

Thoughts or prayers for healing must be followed by thoughts of the individual's daily activities being resumed. We must use our imaginations and "see" him becoming a part of his family and society again. The patient must become a person once more. It is just as easy to imagine or visualize the sick person as up and about, performing his daily tasks, as it is to visualize him lying in bed. After all, the former state of life is far more natural than the latter one. And all images of the person performing his household chores serve to deepen our faith in the healing process. More, they help the sick one to realize his return to health also.

How can prayer or thought of another heal the one who is ill? Again, science has not provided us with answers, but historical evidence abounds that one person may indeed heal another by becoming the channel through which the healing energy of faith can flow freely. Modern-day evidence concerning this is not lacking either. It comes from such reliable sources as Unity School of Christianity, Christian Science, Ambrose and Olga Worral, Katherine Kuhlman, and others of unquestionable integrity.

It seems reasonable to believe that the power of the Creator works through each of his creations in an identical way, and hence we are able to help each other in times of distress. There are those times, of course, when people of deep faith in being healed have failed to demonstrate the healing. On the surface it may have seemed to an observer that all the conditions for healing were in working order. But this is an external appearance only, and it must be remembered that what seems to be and what really is may be different. No man today may fully know the inmost feelings and thoughts of another. Instruments are not made which can measure them for us. However, work toward this goal is being done.

Dr. William Tiller[2] has laid a hypothesis for this in stating his belief that thought is a form of electrical energy and that there may possibly be a fourth circulatory system of an electrical nature which in time may reveal the symptoms of disease before they are manifested in physical form. When the time comes that such a hypothesis is demonstrated, we will also be able to detect man's most intimate thoughts and feelings.

If this hypothesis can be accepted, it will be much easier to see why faith plays such a dynamic role in our thoughts and feelings. No one questions the power of a 10,000-volt current. Is our own thought that powerful? Yes, and ten times more so. Thought—and our faith in our own thoughts—is the steering wheel of our life as well as the power drive.

A realization of this truth would prevent much of our illness. Teachers of spiritual truth all state categorically that illness begins first in the spiritual body, which is invisible to us, with negative thinking and feeling. According to some of the foremost spiritual teachers of our time—Charles Fillmore of Unity; Emmet Fox, author of many books on thought and its results; Ambrose and Olga Worral of Spiritual Fellowship Frontiers; and Edgar Cayce of the Association for Research and Enlightenment—negative thinking destroys our health. It does many other disastrous things in our lives too. They tell us that thoughts of fear, jealousy, greed, envy, hatred, and so on tear down the body. This of course may not happen instantaneously, any more than healing may occur that way. But it does happen because of the inseparable linkage of thought, the central nervous system, and the hormones of the endocrine system from the adrenal, thyroid, and pituitary glands.

As we think, we are, Shakespeare said. Realizing this great truth and applying it in our daily lives requires discipline of every thought, the actual choosing of the thoughts and feelings we will let become part of our lives. This is not child's play. It means that we must be totally honest with ourselves about the thoughts and feelings we have toward others. More, it demands of us that we practice the Golden Rule with every thought and feeling, no matter what others do to us. Few are willing to pay so great a price for good health. It is easier to be ill and let the doctor prescribe a pill or two.

But while we are bedridden and in pain, our thoughts turn to the desire for health once more. We begin planning what we will do when we get well again. And so, with all the negative thinking and self-damage inflicted on ourselves by our wrong thinking, God has provided us a way to return to health through faith built in as part of our thought process.

In summary, then, faith is a belief in the occurrence of a condition or situation to come about without visible proof that it will actually do so. Faith is a component of every thought and feeling we have, whether or not it is of a religious nature. When healing occurs following thoughts, it is because the individual believes in such healing. This makes man a participant in his own conditions of life.

Thousands of persons have been healed by this thinking-feeling process which totally involves the entire central nervous system, the endocrine glands, and the cells of the body. Evidence of one such healing has been presented for the reader.

When healing occurs instantly we tend to think of it as a miracle, instead of understanding that a miracle is only a happening for which we must find the laws of operation.

7

Faith Makes the Difference

BY JUDITH CORRENTI, R.N.

It's faith I want to write about. This faith is of a divine source. A special strength is contained in this faith which helps us to go through a difficult illness. Although God does not send adversity and sickness our way, he uses them to fulfill his perfect plan for the Christian's life. We become very humble in our weakened state, as we see our own smallness in the world and our utter dependence upon God. When it seems as though we have nothing else to offer to God he willingly accepts our pain—mental and physical—as the only gifts we have to give. Even these unappealing gifts can be used to give us peace of mind, knowing that nothing comes to us in our lives except via Christ.

In God's time healing will come. The uphill road in the pursuit of health and wholeness may be a long and difficult one through the complicated medical maze. But be comforted in the knowledge that we are never alone in this battle. Christ has walked each step of the journey before us. He has given man miraculous abilities to aid the healing process. Faith knows that God's powers far exceed man's. When science reaches the end of its capabilities, God begins rapidly accelerating the healing process.

This faith hastens recovery and alleviates mental and physical pain by diminishing fear. Fear and panic about ourselves is replaced by a serene peace that only comes from God. Fear is more lethal than any disease. Patience replaces panic, and we can look ahead and encourage others when it seems as though there is nothing left to hope for in the future.

Faith allows us to cope with our problems, knowing that God really cares for us and understands our deepest anxieties and our hidden desires. Faith enables one to look beyond today's pain and limitations to a future free of these problems. It is knowing that every dark and painful day ends, giving way to a serene restoration of mind and body in peaceful sleep. With faith in God securely intact, one has the ability to control his disease rather than allowing the disability to paralyze mind and spirit.

Last and most importantly, faith is knowing that even when our life on earth ends, we will be given eternal life free of all illness. I find this to be true in my own life as I have battled a difficult disease. And as a nurse, I've seen it work for others.

8

Divine Physician

BY IMOGENE KASERMAN, R.N.

The baby's screams of pain and fright dragged me back from the black abyss of exhausted sleep. Looking at the horribly burned little back, I saw several areas of fresh bleeding where the baby had scraped against the crib bars. I could only think, She can't live—don't they know she's going to die?

My next thought was one of severe condemnation. I had been asleep. Asleep with a dying baby who needed me. Asleep on duty!

I am a registered nurse. The R.N. means far more than a license to me; it is a commitment. When I was a small child, "Nurse" was my favorite game. I could always find something sick to nurse or mother.

Then came the years of strict and demanding training in a general hospital. The discipline of those years developed the virtues of total dependability and complete acceptance of the Florence Nightingale Pledge. I was appalled to find that I had dozed off. I was shocked at my negligence.

The baby's mother! She had trusted me with her little darling. Apparently she didn't realize how serious this burn was. Why hadn't someone told her? How could I ever face her? I couldn't! I just shouldn't stay on duty. I was unworthy of my uniform, cap, and the hospital pin that reads: *Deo per homines servire*. I had failed the mother and I had failed myself—all that I had ever been or promised to become.

Glancing out the window, I saw and felt the serenity of the beautiful moonlight night. I seemed to experience a flood of quiet confidence as I moved toward that window. Climbing up on the ledge, I opened the window in order to go outside toward the source of peace and calm. It seemed the right thing to do. It seemed the only thing to do.

Then the cool night air brought full consciousness—and even greater shock and self-condemnation. I turned from the peace of the night to move to the crib to pick up Jenny—my own baby.

In the two days and nights since her burns she had become accustomed to my holding her by grasping the back of that curly blond head and the chubby thighs. Other areas of the back and legs were covered with severe burns. No one else had held her during these long hours; my brief sleep had been true exhaustion. However, I couldn't accept this as an excuse.

At the time I only knew that I had nearly jumped from a second-story hospital window. I saw this as a weakness I had not been aware of, a character defect I could not tolerate or accept. I couldn't tell my husband or anyone else. I couldn't even talk to God or plead for his forgiveness, for I felt it was unforgivable. I simply blocked it from my mind for several years.

This experience for me was like a painful tooth that you occasionally explore with a timid tongue. I would very briefly remember the inviting moonlight and puzzle at my desire to jump and the peace that came with my decision. The old stab of self-condemnation brought spiritual pain. I was too shattered by my behavior to attempt to examine the dynamics, to understand or gain any personal insight.

How thankful I am that a day finally came when I could look at myself with some honesty. Only then could I learn about myself *and* other people and begin to grow a little taller spiritually. Only by accepting my personal actions could I understand and accept the behavior of others.

What happened at that open window when I suddenly realized who I was? Why had I lost faith in myself? For I had failed myself in time of crisis. I found that I did not have the strength I had always assumed was unshakable. I could not admit my weakness to myself or tell those closest to me. For don't you know that when we fail ourselves we feel we have failed both our Maker and all who love us?

Jenny was burned . . . seriously burned . . . and she needed her mother. I blocked out my near-suicide attempt. The wonderful people who surrounded my entire family during this crisis supported me with their loving concern and with their constant prayers. They seemed to know our every need and responded before we thought to ask. One of the richest blessings God gives is the love of Christian friends who walk with you when the way is dark.

Dr. Tom Dooley once spoke of the brotherhood of suffering. Although he was referring to the personal experience of physical pain, I have a deep conviction that this brotherhood must embrace a host of us who have watched others suffer and have experienced a deep empathy regardless of kinship or even friendship. I feel that I was taken into this brotherhood of suffering during Jenny's illness. And once you have felt a part of this worldwide concern for the hurts of humanity, you can never quite drop out.

Some came to the hospital and said, "Let me know if there's anything at all I can do to help." Some came with a sandwich and a malt and said, "I can sit with Jenny while she sleeps. You eat and go walk around the block." Each of them brought love and concern. I found that the second group had walked through the valley I was experiencing. I can no longer respond to the hurt of another by casually saying, "I know just how you feel," for I have found there are many heartaches I cannot share. I have learned to say, "Would you like to tell me about it?" and I try to listen with prayerful attention. I listen with my ears and my heart.

Christian friends came, and as they left they assured me of their daily prayers for Jenny's healing. They promised to pray for the doctors who handled the case. They promised to pray that my husband and I would have the physical strength to stay at Jenny's bedside and care for the four older children at home. I know these prayers had power. I saw prayer answered.

The young surgeon who was called in by our pediatrician the night of the accident had not known me as a nurse. Yet he was very kind but honest in talking with me about the extent of Jenny's injuries. This young doctor advised me to make arrangements to stay at the hospital with my baby for four to six weeks. He felt that after that time I would be able to manage her at home until she was ready for skin grafting.

Let me summarize many hours of nursing care into a small nutshell—we were able to take Jenny home after only two weeks, and skin grafts were never necessary. The surgeon made house calls to check her progress. His last visit is still very clear in my mind, for he said, "I'm so glad that you are a nurse. This burn has healed more quickly than I had dreamed possible. I have never had a burn this extensive that did not become infected and that did not require any grafting. Can you explain to me just what you feel were the contributing factors?"

This conversation was years ago. I may not have worded his question exactly, but this was the essence of his thoughts. I feel certain this conversation remains in my thinking because I had spent a great deal of time wondering about Jenny's recovery before his question came. I gave him the answer that I still believe to be true.

I reminded him that we had transferred Jenny from the hospital where I had first taken her to emergency, on the night she was burned, to Children's Hospital for admission and treatment. The nurses had never used anything in her room that had not been carefully sterilized. I can't feel that this was just a lucky coincidence.

Children's Hospital encouraged me to stay right with my baby. She did not feel neglected or rejected. She never cried for me or became frightened that I would leave her. They furnished me a bed and meals and made it possible for me to provide the love and warmth that brought her security.

I saved my most important factor for the last. I looked straight into the doctor's eyes as I reminded him that we were a Christian family and that I had felt guided and sustained throughout the entire illness. I told him that two groups of people that I had not known personally had been meeting each week to pray for Jenny's recovery. I assured him of my appreciation for all that he had done but admitted that I must also give thanks to the Divine Physician.

This doctor smiled and shrugged as he turned to leave. He had said that he couldn't understand Jenny's healing. He still does not understand.

9

Mighty Lourdes and Little Bernadette

BY KARLA COOPER, R.N.

In 1858, little Marie Bernarde Soubirous started an avalanche of reaction to faith in the healing power of prayer that hasn't stopped yet. It was as if the very snow from her own high Pyrenees had begun to slide, encompassing the whole world.

In 1866, eight years later, four-foot seven-inch Bernadette, now Sister Marie-Bernarde in the Convent of Saint-Gildard of the Sisters of Nevers, told the story of seeing her "most beautiful lady" in the dirty cavern at Massabielle while her sister Marie and a friend, Jeanne Abadie, were gathering sticks for firewood across the River Gave. She spoke shyly and briefly, intimidated by the presence of the Mother General and all the rest. Only when she repeated the words of the Blessed Virgin, "I am the Immaculate Conception," was there awed silence. The narrator had told her story hundreds of times, and in the repeating had become matter-of-fact and dry.

By this time, of course, the Bouhouhorts child had long been cured of his near-fatal convulsions by the spring water that had been analyzed several times. Surprisingly enough, it had been found to be similar to the other pure spring waters of the area. The many other unexplainable cures were embarrassing the skeptical authorities of Lourdes.

When a man who had been blind suddenly saw and when a cripple threw down his crutch and walked, free thinkers in Paris wrote, "Hydropaths also claim to obtain marvelous cures by the use of pure water, but they don't pretend they perform miracles!" The spring was running at the rate of 250,000 gallons a day, but important journalists, without bothering to see for themselves, dismissed this as a "trickling of water from the rocks of a grotto."[1]

Today the spring still flows at this rate. Millions of invalids have been to Lourdes, and the medical bureau, an impartial body of physicians of repute, has designated 262 miraculous cures in the forty-one-year span between 1914 and 1955. The ecclesiastical authorities agree with this number. According to Zsolt Aradi:

The "Medical Bureau" has existed since 1884, but even before this date the bishop had organized an official controlling body composed of local doctors. Bernadette's mental soundness had been confirmed by three independent psychiatrists who were ordered to examine her by Baron Massy, the top government official of the district. The present medical bureau works together with an international study center established in 1904. The Medical Bureau has a different function from that of the International Study Center. It examines the sick, keeps records, makes the diagnosis. Further, it follows the course of a visiting patient's disease or cure, and collects data on the patient's family, background and medical history.

The M.B. expresses no opinion on any healing—miraculous or non-miraculous—before the end of the second year after the patient involved has come to Lourdes and claimed to have been cured there. Newspaper accounts of miraculous cures at Lourdes are merely personal descriptions and subjective opinions. The M.B. detailed clinical, scientific verdict is never disclosed before the end of the second year. Then the whole case goes to the bishop, or ordinary of the diocese to which the sick person belongs, and only the bishop can issue a decree declaring a cure miraculous. The I.S.C. assists the visiting physicians, who come from all over the world, and in a way acts as a supervisory body over the M.B. During the existence of the M.B. and the I.S.C., thirty thousand physicians have registered as visitors. The number of physicians who actually work with the M.B. ranges from 800 to 1,500 a year. These two medical institutions are not ecclesiastical or religious bodies. Any doctor of any race, any country, any faith or ideology, has the right to examine the records and raise questions. Only one document is required—the doctor's certified medical diploma. This freedom of access to all records guarantees an absolute openness and increases the value of the medical examinations. If only Catholic doctors were to sign the minutes of the meetings at which cases are discussed, criticisms or suspicions of their objectivity would be justifiable. But non-believing physicians also affix their signatures to these documents.[2]

The word miracles for these instantaneous, unexplainable cures at Lourdes, either after the dipping into the waters, during the processional and blessing, or after the application of the water near the site, is not used; the Medical Bureau has banned this term. Nevertheless, cures are reported around the world after prayer and use of the water, either by the invalid himself or another. The function of the doctors is the function of all scientists—to report and establish the facts.

One of the greatest physicians of France, Alexis Carrel, a Nobel prize winner and author of *Man, the Unknown,* though he was a skeptic who had lost his Catholic faith, was driven by scientific curiosity to go to Lourdes on one of the white trains of invalids. He went with an open mind, expecting to make a fair medical judgment in case an unusual healing occurred while he was there.

He examined, wrote up his own case history, and followed with the keenest interest the progress of a woman whom attendants on the train and Carrel himself doubted would ever survive long enough even to reach the southern French city. She was almost in extremis when laved in the pool, and the attendants there were most reluctant to immerse her, as is usually the custom, so her abdomen alone was bathed. At the Grotto, Carrel stayed as close to her as possible, doubting, wanting to see the Hand of God for his own soul's sake but being judiciously scientific throughout.

This woman had had tuberculosis of the lung in her early youth, but she had been halfway cured. At the time of her arrival in Lourdes she had peritonitis of tubercular origin. Carrel describes the next happening matter-of-factly in his *Voyage to Lourdes.* He states that it seemed to him the features of the invalid suddenly changed and her usual pallor decreased. But the doctor did not want to believe his eyes. Perhaps he was hallucinating, though he certainly hadn't been up to that time. He took her pulse and told another doctor nearby that her respirations were slower. His colleague replied in a resigned tone that she was dying. Carrel did not answer him. He knew this time something had happened.

Before his very eyes, the condition of this moribund woman quickly and visibly started to change. He studied her constantly. The change of her face, which was fixed on the Grotto, was undeniable. The doctor felt his own face pale as he watched the blanket drop which covered the woman's abdomen. In a very few moments, it seemed to him, the large abdominal tumor disappeared. He came closer to her and asked her how she felt, observing her respirations and neck at the same time. She told him she felt very well, not strong, but convinced she was cured. She was offered milk which she drank easily and with no trouble. She then raised her head and turned over on her side unassisted and with no sign of pain.

Carrel visited her in the evening and found her sitting up in bed. Her eyes shone and her face, though still thin and haggard, reflected life and there was color in her cheeks. Her respirations were normal, her pulse 80, and she was full of confidence. The doctor lifted the blanket and observed her abdomen. It was normal. He palpated it, but the woman felt no pain. All signs of the tumor were absolutely gone.

Carrel visited the Basilica that night. He was well aware that he had to come to some decision. He didn't doubt that a miracle had happened, for this was beyond all scope of a human, scientific explanation. But just how far-reaching a miracle had occurred, he had yet to find out. He went into the Basilica and knelt down to pray.

Suddenly, after sitting motionless for a long time with his face in his hands, a prayer to the Blessed Virgin, to Bernadette's "most beautiful Lady," burst from his soul. He prayed to believe blindly, if need be, for his intellectual pride was still deep and hard. He clutched a dream of believing in her, and he promised to try and love her as those pure in heart did.

By the time he got back to his room, he seemed to have cleared away any lingering doubts and he was at peace with the wonderful—literally, "full of wonder"—miracle of healing he had been privileged to witness.

What is it then at mighty Lourdes that attracts millions of people each year? In 1954, about two years before Aradi's book, *The Book of Miracles,* was published, four million pilgrims visited the Grotto. Little Bernadette's unwavering love for her "Lady," whom no one else ever did see, inspired such faith in the others who came with her to say the rosary and honor our Blessed Mother that they were more than ready to make an avowal of belief in the apparitions long before the church held its lengthy investigation and declared the apparitions of Lourdes worthy of belief. History has repeated itself many, many times in this regard. Our Lady has been God's instrument so very many times to help his people in their afflictions that mortals yearn for a confirmation of their faith and an answer to their prayers. Who of us does not want a miracle, a tangible proof that our hopes and faith are important enough so that God will manifest his divine will and heal as Christ did so many times in New Testament days?

You may recall that when Bernadette went hesitantly to Dean Peyramale to give him Our Lady's message (she was, after all, only a little girl overawed by the stern Dean), he demanded that she tell the Blessed Virgin he wanted a miracle performed—i.e., that his roses bloom in February—before he would consider any processions being allowed to honor her at the Grotto. But Mary is not without a sense of humor, and the spring she caused to bubble up from the ground of Massabielle could water all the roses of the world for as long as the world lasts. Her spring was to be like the Pool of Bethesda which the angel of the Lord stirred and the first person immersed was cured. And yet, the spring of Lourdes was to be different. For after Bernadette dug a little into the ground for it at her Lady's instructions, and drank from it and washed herself, it was to be "stirred" eternally and be available for anyone's cure at God's will.

And the roses of the abbé: well, I don't think the good abbé realized what he asked for, because my daughter and I saw roses blooming there, not far from the Grotto, in January of 1972—a whole bed of yellow roses, in bud, full bloom, and bloomed out—and I touched them in the ground in which they grew. Granted that France, especially southern France, near the Spanish border, has a milder climate than ours, but roses in January? And we saw the flames on the huge votive candles, swept at a 45-degree angle by the strong, snow-chilled winds from the Pyrenees, still burning night and day, never going out till the candle itself was burned out. Was it a miracle the abbé wanted? It seems to me one should be rather careful when one demands something of heaven. One just might get more than one expects!

Our visit to Lourdes was not during the "season," i.e., between May and October, when the white trains (so-called because all the nurses and attendants wear white) bring in invalids from all over Europe. Regrettably, we missed this and the wonderful and inspiring processions, the blessing of the sick, and the countless vocalized rosaries which storm heaven for help for the afflicted. To read about it—the invocations of thousands of voices chanting "Lord, that I may see!" or "Lord, help me to walk!" or "Lord, that I may hear!"—is inspiring; so must the people have called after Christ when he walked the earth. To actually hear it must stir the very soul.

All nationalities, all tongues, the rich, the poor, the privileged, the underprivileged, all the same in the age-old plea for mitigation of the ills of body and soul, for who shall say there is no interplay between them? Much has been written about perfectionists getting ulcers; about incurable worriers getting stomach trouble; about nonrelaxers succumbing to heart attacks; about certain types of people being more susceptible to cancer, to TB, to sinus, chest, and respiratory diseases; about accident-prone people who constantly fracture, cut, or dislocate this or that.

So we have Lourdes and its God-instigated cures, and we have the faith of the people of the world who come or send for water from its pool and use it with confidence. Not all are cured at Lourdes, only a few. But as it has been said a hundred times, no one comes away unchanged.

10

The Value of Christian Commitment in the Experiences of Stress and Illness

BY MARGARET E. ARMSTRONG, R.N., M.S., PH.D.,
AND JEAN R. MILLER, R.N., M.A.

Is life easier for the person committed to the principles of living taught by Christ? Does the Christian encounter fewer problems and experience less illness than others? Is he perhaps as vulnerable as those around him but better able to cope with the problems and benefit from the effects of suffering and ill health? These questions have puzzled mankind for centuries.

There have been numerous accounts of persons who have experienced far less illness after committing their lives to Christ. And it is possibly true that in general the person growing in and manifesting God's gifts of peace, joy, and love is also less susceptible to the stressors which cause various types of illness. However, one only needs to look to the experiences of the apostle Paul to realize that even the most committed of Christians experienced many problems and ordeals. And when we look into ourselves, although we may note that some periods of our lives have been relatively free of illness, few if any of us have sustained a closeness to God which has kept us in continual good health.

Considering these facts, it would seem to be helpful to look into scripture for specific and practical suggestions for the times when we are anticipating, experiencing, or attempting to recover from the effects of various types of stress and illness. The kinds and interrelationships of stressors and illnesses which we commonly experience will be discussed in this chapter. The ways in which God protects us from the results of these experiences will then be considered, as well as the process and effects of healing.

Problems inherent in living vary in their nature and magnitude, but they are all potential sources of stress which may alone or in various combinations cause many problems, one of the most common being illness. The type, number, and amount of stressors that will cause ill health vary among individuals and from time to time with the same person.

Problems of a psychological or social nature are numerous and originate from factors inherent in our culture, childhood, interrelationships, and environment. Our self-image may be threatened by an event resulting in a sense of helplessness, isolation, or insecurity. Financial problems and the consequent inability to provide the desired living standard for oneself or one's family often produces frustration, loss of self-confidence, and illness. Unresolved conflicts between members of the family or co-workers can cause an unlimited number of psychological and emotional problems. With the increased tempo of living and rate of change in the technology of today, the pressures of succeeding and adapting not only have increased the incidence of some illnesses but have also resulted in illness, such as coronary heart disease, that were relatively unknown decades ago.

We are also subject to such physical stressors as viruses, adverse weather conditions, and accidents associated with travel, recreation, and work. Presently, we are finding heretofore unknown or ignored physical stressors resulting from disposal of industrial wastes, the use of pesticides, and other yet-to-be-discovered sources.

In the spiritual realm of our lives, we continually seem to fall short of our expectations in one way or another. Frustration, guilt, and loss of confidence sometimes result. Causal relationships between spiritual problems and illness are frequently so subtle that they are often not identified or eliminated. Facing temptations of various types is one of the more common sources of spiritual stressors. Scripture states: So the man who thinks he can stand must be on his guard against a fall. It is no superhuman temptation that you have had. And God can be depended on not to let you be tried beyond your strength, but when temptation comes, to give you a way out of it, so that you can withstand it. (See 1 Corinthians 10:12–13.)

Space does not permit a complete discussion of the characteristics of the various stressors which influence our health. It is important to realize that any type of problem can contribute to the formation of any of several forms of illness. In other words, an emotional stressor such as the need to meet production quotas in a job can be a causal factor leading to a peptic ulcer but may also cause an emotional or spiritual illness.

It has been shown that nearly any important life change increases the probability of illness, and when several changes occur close together, the probability is even higher.[1] Some of the more influential changes include the death of a spouse, divorce, a jail term, marriage, and retirement. To be viewed comprehensively, we must look at ourselves as spiritual, emotional, and physical beings, exposed to stresses of all types which are capable of affecting us in any one or all of these major aspects.

For the purposes of this discussion, let us assume that Christians and non-Christians alike are exposed to similar stresses in daily life. If this is the case, then, it is hoped, God provides assistance in coping with stressful experiences to reduce the probability of illness or, in the event of illness, to permit the person to benefit as much as possible from the effects of the illness.

In discussing illness, one may immediately think of the healing power of God as being directed toward the cure of an existing disease. The occurrence of this type of healing is covered in more detail in other portions of this book. It is pertinent to the present discussion to note that Christ demonstrated God's healing power in curing both physical illness, as in the case of the woman with a bleeding problem of twelve years' duration (Matthew 9:21), and a combination of an emotional and spiritual illness for the man possessed with demons (Luke 8:36). From these and other scriptural examples, as well as present-day healing experiences, it is evident that God can provide healing for all the various types of stresses and resulting illnesses.

It is often overlooked that God also provides healing and protection in the prevention of illness by assisting the individual to deal effectively with occurring problems. His healing powers also include protection from the adverse effects of illness which do occur. This type of "healing" is available in many forms and is, like the curing of disease, related to all types of stressors and illnesses.

The fear of impending danger is a common occurrence for most of us. Hence, scripture provides us with many accounts of

Christ's reducing the fear of those in peril as well as providing protection against the danger itself. Jesus stilled the waters when the disciples were afraid during a storm (Matthew 8:25). As Peter began to sink when he looked away from Christ while walking to him on the water, Christ immediately saved him (Matthew 14:30). We are even admonished to resist worrying about adequate clothing and food (Matthew 6:25-34), the lack of which certainly appears to be a danger to many of us. It does not seem that the Christian is immune from all dangers, but God's protection does provide us with appreciable security from fear no matter what we are experiencing (Romans 1:16-17). One may also recall instances in which God has prevented an impending danger from occurring or has rendered an otherwise dangerous event harmless.

The world is full of potential dangers, but man is protected with a continual healing power against the perils inherent in any generation, just as in the early days of the church (Acts 2:40). Barclay describes this power as a "kind of divine antiseptic which keeps him from infection by the evil of the world."[2]

The feeling of being isolated, alone, or lost is commonly described by individuals as one of the stresses of living. The feeling of aloneness during the occurrence of a problem often makes us unable to cope or work toward an effective solution. We are more willing to allow ourselves to be passive or to ignore or retreat from the stressor. The responses may lead to many adverse effects, frequently including illness. But God tells us that we are never truly alone in that he is always with us (Matthew 28:20). Indeed, it was the lost and alone that Christ came to save (Matthew 18:11 and Luke 19:10). A drastic decrease in the feeling of lostness and aloneness is often noted by persons describing changes in their lives following their initial or renewed commitment to Christ. This assurance of protection inherent in the constant companionship of God is certainly an asset in times of crisis and frequently provides the necessary edge of confidence and calmness required for effective coping with the stress at hand.

Protection from the effects of sin and sin itself is also a type of God's healing power that is available to us. We often recognize the sinful nature of an act or object and are aware of the adverse effects of becoming involved with the activity in question. However, left to our own resources, we are often unable to determine the appropriate solution to avoid the problem altogether or, if that is not possible, to eliminate its adverse results. Fortunately, God protects us from many of these sins if we let him, and he often renders us safe from the negative effects of unavoidable or unknowing sins (Matthew 1:21).

We sometimes forget that the salvation given to us by the death and resurrection of Christ protects and heals us from the wrath of God which we would otherwise be fully subject to through our own nature and acts (Romans 5:9). This fact is so important and extensive to our entire life as Christians that we find it difficult to realize its impact on all facets of living. If our Christian experience did not include this monumental act of healing on the part of God, we would have immeasurably more difficulty in surviving major crises, not to mention the cumulative effect of stresses encountered daily. This source of healing is probably one of God's most frequently ignored gifts, perhaps because it seems so self-evident and obvious in Christian teaching.

It is not possible here to discuss and illustrate fully the various types of healing provided to us by God. By surveying one's experiences and needs, it is possible, however, to realize that each type of healing is required to provide assistance, protection, and other tools needed to avoid or cope with the many types of stressors and illnesses inherent in living in society today. Because God's salvation and healing powers are eschatological—that is, are timeless in their nature and effect—we can receive as much benefit from utilizing these powers today as in the times described by scripture (Romans 13:11; 1 Corinthians 5:5; 2 Timothy 4:18; 1 Peter 1:5).

God provides us with some additional reminders which can assist us in obtaining any of these types of healing. As already mentioned, it is vital to remember that God is always with us (Matthew 28:20). This reminder then leads us to be better able to follow further advice given during both Old and New Testament times. We are told to take courage even in times of peril and to not be afraid (Matthew 14:22-23, 27). We are not to allow our faith to waver (Matthew 14:31). No source of harm, including that originating from other people, is supposed to be capable of provoking fear within us (Psalms 23:4; 27:7). No matter what the circumstances, we are told that we must not be troubled or have *any* anxiety (John 14:1; Philippians 4:6-7).

These scriptural passages are familiar to many of us and sound very positive and beneficial. But how many of us achieve this level of optimism and calmness in daily problems, much less under the occasional more threatening stressor that we all experience? It would seem that precious few are capable of achieving this feat. The results are seen in the increasing number and percentage of illnesses, the origin of which can be traced to the inability to avoid or adapt to stress of one type or another. Perhaps this is why so much scripture is devoted to describing the sources of help available from God.

When and if we are able to reach out of our desire to control our lives to these healing powers from God, we find that not only is there little value in being anxious and fearful but that we are better able effectively to avoid or cope with the problem at hand. The development of this ability to remain calm and act effectively in a crisis of any magnitude involves a lifelong endeavor on our part. However, we can, with constant effort and reminding, gradually increase our reliance on God's protective and healing powers in order either to do nothing or take effective action, whichever is appropriate.

First of all, it does help to be aware of the types of help available from God. Second, we need to develop our unique ways of acquiring this help. Many of us are inclined to want a specific formula to use in order to acquire whatever we feel is needed. We forget or do not place value on the fact that we are each unique in God's creative pattern and we are given the freedom by God to utilize our gifts and abilities to avail ourselves of his healing powers. Because of this unique individual nature and freedom, scripture provides us with suggestions of a general character which can be modified according to our individual makeup and need.

The nature and maturity of our faith and our ability to communicate with God are certainly two important aspects to consider in availing ourselves of God's healing powers. Faith is a gift from God which, by its nature as a gift, needs to be opened, utilized, and matured by and not for us. Much is said about faith in scripture, and a periodic, detailed study of this gift would certainly be of value to all of us. In thinking about healing, faith is needed initially to hear and believe what God has to say about the types of healing available from him. We also need faith to believe that God allows only what we can bear and will give us the strength to bear whatever he allows to occur (1 Corinthians 10:12-13). We stumble in appropriating these promises when the nature or amount of our faith does not allow us to fully believe these promises or to obtain and use the help available from God.

Nearly everything we say and do as Christians has an effect upon the nature of our faith. We must be constantly on guard to avoid or minimize influences which will tend to decrease or degrade our faith and to seek experiences and activities which will increase and mature that faith.

It is also vital to continue to evaluate the balance of the major components of our faith, insofar as our emotions, soul, and mind are concerned. For surely, if we are to love our God with our emotions, soul, and mind, then this also tells us that our faith should also involve these three aspects (Matthew 22:37). At times, upon checking, we will find that the growth in our faith and our closeness to God has been hindered, perhaps because we have been on an "intellectual or philosophical trip," emphasizing intellectual activities at the expense of time and energy allotted to our emotional relationship with God. At other times, we may find that we have indulged ourselves emotionally with God without seeking an appropriate increase in our knowledge or wisdom of God's teaching.

Though it is often difficult, we will find much value in continually assessing the balance of our thoughts, activities, and components of our faith in God. We can see examples of this value in many lives. As with Abraham, only when we are emotionally close to God can we fully hear his messages, feel his guidance, and then believe that what we hear is truly from him. Within the working of our soul, we can then will to commit ourselves to this teaching and guidance. We may act upon that commitment, even in times of uncertainty, but always with confidence. As a result, our faith increases and matures evermore, enabling us to be better able to hear, believe, make a commitment, and act. As we continually assess the balance of our faith, we are able to stay within this divine cycle provided by God to mature us as Christians.

Communicating with God in the form of prayer has many forms and purposes. How and why we pray must be determined by each of us according to our relationship with God, our individuality, and the nature of the situation. We are admonished to avoid worrying but, instead, to pray about everything, telling God our needs and not forgetting to thank him for his answers (Philippians 14:6).

Two ideas seem to be evident from the aforementioned scripture. We can pray or communicate with God about anything, and we should always give thanks for his answers. This means that a stressor or problem can be neither too trivial nor too immense to pray about it. As Barclay so aptly states, "We can pray for forgiveness for the past, for the things we need in the present, and for help and guidance for the future, with all our shame, with all our needs, with all our fears, into the presence of God."[3]

Being thankful while one prays implies a sincere feeling of gratitude for everything that comes from God. Also implied is a submission, hopefully growing toward perfection, to the will of God. We should strive to "know that in everything God works for good with those who love him, who are called according to his purpose (Rom. 8:28)." Here, the interdependence between faith and prayer begins to become evident. For only through an ever maturing and encompassing faith can we meaningfully pray about everything, discern what is from and of God's will, be thankful, and benefit from his answers. At times we fall short at the point of realizing that his answer is not what we desired. We then may be so disappointed, confused, or bitter that we do not remain close enough to God to recognize what his desired outcomes are for our lives. We have to be able to recognize what we are to learn and how we are to be affected by the stressor within the framework of God's will.

Whatever type of God's healing is experienced, the results for the individual are geared to his or her specific needs at the time. The immediate objective of the healing, at least for the individual, is effective coping or elimination of the stressor at hand. More often than not, there are other benefits resulting from the healing beyond this immediate goal. It seems that God usually has a greater purpose in exposing us to stress and allowing us to suffer in any way.

Scripture describes several psychological and spiritual benefits when one encounters and conquers stress through God's healing. For instance, we come to increase our possession of fortitude, patience, and joy (Colossians 1:9-11). Fortitude can be thought of as a victorious type of patience which is demonstrated when we have the ability to endure problems and turn them into glory. It is the ability to deal triumphantly with any stressor that life contains. The joy is an everpresent, impregnating happiness which pervades the darkest of life's moments and is made possible by the knowledge of God's presence, love, and guidance in any situation.

The term patience as used in this scriptural passage can be thought of as a type of long-suffering. It is a spirit which never loses patience with, belief in, or hope for men. The development of this type of patience, then, has the potential of leading to strength of character, which in turn can lead to a greater trust in God. This increasing trust can then lead to a stronger and more steady faith and hope. This enhances the ability of the individual to hold steadfast and confident, regardless of what happens, as the Holy Spirit fills us with God's love.

Here, we have, if we allow God's will to take its course, another cyclic way of coping with life's problems and growing as Christians at the same time. For the experience of a problem leads to patience and sequentially to strength of character, trust in God, strong and steady faith and hope, greater confidence no matter what the circumstance, and a greater fulfillment of God's love. This results in an increased ability to work through a problem of even greater magnitude, and the sequence may repeat itself, with the end result being the attainment of a higher level of strength and coping ability.

One of the additional results of allowing oneself to benefit fully from the results of God's healing is greater peace of mind. This is certainly a free gift from God which can be increased with successful experiences with the stresses of life. For Christ said, "I am leaving you with a gift . . . peace of mind and heart! And the peace I give you is not fragile like the peace the world gives, so don't be troubled or afraid." (See John 14:27.) It seems that the peace intended for us from God is not meant to be a possession that wanes or disappears in times of stress, but which remains steady at these times to assist us in calmly and effectively dealing with the problem. It is far more difficult to think, much less act, effectively and appropriately when we are fearful or anxious.

It seems that all the fruits of the Spirit—that is, love, joy, peace, patience, kindness, goodness, faithfulness, gentleness, and self-control—are potentially enhanced as a result of the types of healing which God provides (Galatians 5:22-23). The enhancement of this spiritual and emotional "set" will have physiological effects as well. For reasons not yet fully understood, these characteristics seem to render an individual less susceptible to various types of illnesses. The comparatively tense, depressed, or impatient person tends to fall prey to more frequent and, at times, more severe physical and psychological pathologies. Thus the total being may benefit from allowing God to manifest his healing in whatever form is needed.

The emphasis of this discussion has not been in relation to God's healing in the most common sense of the term—that is, the curing of an existing disease. Rather, the types of stressors and illnesses which we experience during life and the other ways in which God can heal have been described. Thus, in addition to curing a disease, God heals by eliminating or minimizing the harmful effects of stress and by enabling us to cope with problems, which often results in the prevention of illness. Should an illness occur, God may not only heal the disease itself but also may heal us from the adverse effects of the experience. Whatever the type of healing that God employs, his purpose is usually more far-reaching in our lives than the healing itself. The results of God's healing can reach into the innermost fabric of our being to stimulate further growth as Christians. This renders us better able to cope with the stresses of life with a healthy spirit, soul, and body and with evermore increasing thanksgiving and praise of God.

III

11

Healing and Salvation: A Clinical View (Implications of Recent Studies in Healing Time After Retinal Detachment Surgery)

BY THE REV. ROBERT B. REEVES, JR.

Some years ago, an eye surgeon specializing in detached retina repair reviewed several hundred of his cases and found a 400 percent difference in healing time between the most rapid and the least rapid healers. Healing time was taken to be the number of days from the surgery to the reappearance of pigmentation in the retina, which is a sign of the completion of the process of reattachment and recovery of vision in the affected area. The normal range of variance in similar biological processes is 18 to 20 percent.

About that time, the surgeon became acquainted with the chaplain, and he began to ask the chaplain to see some of his patients. One woman on whom he had operated had been so tense before surgery that she required an extraordinarily large amount of anesthetic. The operation was a failure. Before he operated again, the surgeon had the chaplain see the woman daily for a week. Little by little, she began talking out her fears and anxieties, until at the end of the week she was relaxed enough to go to sleep without medication for the first time in months. For the second operation, she needed the smallest amount of anesthetic in the surgeon's experience, and she healed afterward very rapidly.

Another female patient had not begun to heal six days after surgery; her eye was just as it had been when she left the operating room. Finding in the night nurse's notes some indications of emotional distress, the surgeon asked the chaplain to see her. The chaplain did so the same day, but to no avail; the woman simply shut him out with chitchat. When he saw her the next day she began the same way, but suddenly her voice broke and for an hour she poured forth an almost incredible tale of bitterness, hatred, fear, and guilt. Nearly every close relationship she had ever known had become poisoned. The morning following, the surgeon called the chaplain to tell him that overnight the patient had caught up in her healing; her eye was as it should be at that time.

These cases, and a good many other less dramatic ones, on top of the 400 percent difference in healing times that the surgeon had earlier observed, required some kind of explanation. So the surgeon, Dr. Graham Clark, and I, the chaplain, agreed to do a study. We obtained a grant from the Rosenwald Family Fund, engaged a second chaplain, Randall Mason, to work entirely on this one project, and built a research team that over an eight-year period at one time or another involved three nurses, two technicians, a psychiatrist, a clinical psychologist, and a third chaplain, in addition to the surgeon and myself.

Scientific Correlation: The Acceptance Scale

During those years over 500 retinal detachment patients were studied. The first 116 cases were analyzed for physiological factors that might correlate with speed of healing: age, sex, severity of damage, type and extent of surgery, type and degree of anesthesia, body chemistry, presence or absence of other diseases. Nothing of significance was turned up. Physiologically the difference could not be explained in terms of factors that could be measured.

So we were faced with what seemed to be a psychological X factor which at first, for lack of better words, we labeled negatively as anxiety, and positively as peace of mind. But how to pin it down in observational categories, how to measure it, and how to test it were for a long time quite beyond us.

The next 200 patients were "trial horses" for an almost endless series of attempts to define the psychological X factor. As far as we could determine, no study like this had ever been done, so there were no established research methods, tests, or instruments that we could use. The problem was further complicated by the requirement that whatever the chaplain did could not be allowed to alter the normal pastoral role of the chaplain in his relationship to patients. He could not use questionnaires, or take notes in the presence of patients, or otherwise contaminate the relationship. One after another of our approaches led into blind alleys. The concepts of anxiety and peace of mind had to be discarded, along with many others that could not be either objectively defined or systematically observed.

In the meantime, I was doing another study, of a group of terminal cancer patients, to see if there were significant factors associated with their acceptance or their denial of the prospect of death. I had found a number of behavioral and attitudinal responses that seemed to indicate acceptance, and I suggested to the retinal detachment study group the possibility that this might offer a clue to the psychological X factor. So we began to spell it out. How well does the patient accept himself, his retinal detachment, the surgery, his surgeon, the hospital situation, the fact that this is a world in which things like retinal detachment happen? How well does he come to terms with these things? Does he say "yes" or "no" to life? Can he take this experience into his world of meaning and go on?

Gradually, somewhere between the 300th and 400th patient, an acceptance scale began to take shape. It went through many stages of revision and refinement and, in its final form, covered a five-point range:

    I. Accepts Totally
   II. Accepts Cautiously
  III. Accepts with Reservation
  IV. Accepts with Resignation
   V. Rejects

This range was placed across the top of the scale. Then a list of observational categories was developed. Ten were found to be the most reliable and were placed along the side of the scale:

1. Reaction to Detachment
2. Reaction to Surgeon
3. Reaction to Surgery
4. Reaction to Chaplain
5. Reaction to Others
6. Coping Ability
7. Self-care Ability
8. Self-image
9. Conversational Style
10. Philosophy of Evil

A patient with a high acceptance rating would thus be one

who was appropriately frightened by the damage to his eye, was confronting the danger, and was willing to do whatever was necessary to remedy the situation. He trusted his surgeon. He was optimistic about the outcome of the operation and yet confident of his ability to cope with reality and redefine his life if the surgery did not succeed. Toward others—patients, staff, and visitors—he was open and friendly; there was a welcome mat at his door. He was glad to have the chaplain as a visitor and enjoyed thoughtful exchanges with him. He appeared to be at home with himself and under no need to project an image. He took care of himself willingly, so far as his condition warranted, and was glad to accept the help of others when his condition required. He could converse in depth and showed a nice sense of humor. He took the bad with the good in life, asked no favors, and when he prayed it was simply for strength to meet his troubles or for grace to accept whatever a day might bring.

At the opposite extreme of low acceptance or rejection was the patient who was reduced to panicky, back-to-the-wall fear by the damage to his sight. He was suspicious and distrustful of his surgeon, pessimistic about the outcome of the operation, and despairing of ever being able to cope if his sight were not restored. He had the bars up against all others in the hospital. He resented the chaplain; if he wanted anything of him at all, it was to demand imperiously that the chaplain put the screws on God through prayer or sacrament. He seemed to be utterly miserable with himself, sulking and angry over his dependence. He refused to do anything for himself and made impatient demands on staff and visitors. He avoided talk and resented any suggestion of humor. The way God had dealt with him was a dirty trick.

These were the extremes. In between were gradations. The scale was marked after the chaplain or another member of the study team had seen the patient. The patient met the observers in the usual course of their duties and thus did not know that he was being rated.

Acceptance and Healing

Forms of this acceptance were tested with the last 100 patients to be studied, in groups of fifty. With the first group of fifty, a rather complicated version of the scale was used. Five different people each made acceptance ratings, and the surgeon rated healing time. Each case was discussed by the entire study group at the time the ratings were made in an effort to clarify the categories of observation. When the series was completed and the ratings were fed into a computer, the correlations between acceptance level and speed of healing came out so high that we suspected we had influenced each other's judgment.

So for the second group of fifty, we simplified the scale to its present form, engaged another chaplain, Bruce Wagner (who had no previous knowledge of the study), moved the study to another hospital, and eliminated all discussion of cases between surgeon and chaplain so that neither knew how the other was rating the patients. At the end of the series, the chaplain's ratings of acceptance and the surgeon's ratings of healing time were fed into a computer, and correlations between high acceptance and rapid healing, at one extreme, and low acceptance and slow healing, at the other extreme, came out at a level of $p = .001$, or one chance in a thousand that the results were due to chance.

This study was published in *The Journal of Religion and Health*,[2] and the acceptance scale is being tested in several other areas. At one medical center a radiologist had found that about 50 percent of the patients with Hodgkin's disease treated with radiation responded favorably, but he could not tell in advance which ones they would be. So he and the chaplain there are applying the acceptance scale to see if it has predictive value for this use of radiotherapy. At another medical center, a hand surgeon and the chaplain are testing the scale to see if there are correlations between acceptance ratings and speed of return of function after hand surgery. At still another center, a surgeon and a chaplain are testing the scale in connection with the healing of abdominal wounds. And here at Presbyterian Hospital, we are hoping to apply the scale in connection with other studies that are soon to get under way.

The beauty of this scale is that it can be used by anyone. Medical, psychological, or religious sophistication is not required. In fact, the most consistently accurate acceptance ratings made by anyone in this whole eight-year project were those made by the eye surgeon's office secretary, on the basis of the conversations she had with patients when they first came to see the doctor!

Acceptance as a Bridge Concept

In discussing the implications of these results, the first thing to be pointed out—most emphatically—is that *no causal relationship may be inferred*. The acceptance scale may be predictive, but the behavioral and attitudinal responses it measures may not be said to be the cause of either slow or rapid healing. Prediction and causation are not the same. One may by certain signs predict the weather, but to say that the signs are the cause of the weather is absurd. Equally absurd would be any claim that the signs which give a high acceptance rating are the cause of rapid healing.

Acceptance is a bridge concept between the totality of an individual's response to danger and the particular phenomenon seen in healing, just as weather signs are a bridge between the totality of forces which influence weather and the particular state of the weather on a given day. If you read the signs correctly, you can tell what the weather is going to be, but the actual forces which produce the weather are something else again.

The second point to be made is a corollary of the first. We cannot say that we are dealing with any sort of "mind-over-body" phenomenon; the results of the use of the acceptance scale *do not* imply that healing is psychogenic or that its speed depends upon psychic factors. All this study shows is that certain behavioral and attitudinal responses are associated with speed of healing—so closely associated, in fact, that they have high predictive value. But it does not show that they speed up or retard healing. I hope you will pardon my stating this so tiresomely, but it must be understood if the whole bearing of the study is not to be betrayed.

The signs that are observed for the acceptance rating and the processes observed for the speed of healing rating are both aspects of the total response a patient makes to a threat to his well-being. Neither is primary; neither is the cause of the other. They are simultaneous and concomitant manifestations of a single ongoing response to danger. High acceptance and rapid healing are simply two different aspects of the same reality, two ways of describing a single phenomenon. Wherever you find a patient whose total response to danger is one that keeps him going on as a whole person, saying "yes" to life, you will find both high acceptance and rapid healing. And wherever you find a patient whose total response to danger is one that leaves him stumbling, bogged down, saying "no" to life, you will find both low acceptance and slow healing. The total response is primary, and both its physical and psychic aspects are derivative and descriptive.

Trust Essential, Piety Problematic

A third disclaimer also must be made. This study has nothing to say about faith healing. It offers no support whatever for the contention that religious faith produces quicker healing. As a matter of fact, some of the quickest healers—those with high acceptance ratings—were avowedly agnostic, if not atheistic. And some of the slowest healers—those with low acceptance ratings—professed to be religious. Among the faiths (patients of all faiths were included in the study) there were no significant differences in either acceptance rating or healing time.

Significant differences were found, however, in the way patients used whatever faith they had and in the way they felt about the occurrence of misfortunes such as retinal detachment. If patients used their faith as a source of strength to face reality and deal with it constructively, they were rapid healers. If they used their faith to hide from reality, or to manipulate or force God's hand, they were slow healers. Those who could accept their detachment, as part of the bad that befalls us along with the good in life, healed well. Those who felt that their detachment was a foul blow, and God a monster for permitting it to happen, healed poorly, if they healed at all.

Far more important than religiosity, therefore, was the basic attitude a patient held toward life. Many who by traditional standards would be classified as nonbelievers showed a far more reverential attitude, a deeper trust, a firmer "yes" to life, than many of the pious who were using their religion to avoid reality and get the rules suspended in their favor. Distrust of life is often masked by frantic piety, and unfortunately many well-meaning people mistake such piety for religion. An honest atheist who has a fundamental trust in life often turns out to be more truly reverential. If such a reverential trust in life is taken as the mark of religious faith, then this study does show that faith and healing go together. But such trust is not what people usually mean when they use the word faith, and therefore I must guard against misinterpretation.

A fourth point to be noted is that in this study we did not deliberately attempt to change a patient's acceptance level. In several instances, when the operation was unsuccessful or when the retina detached a second time, and the patient had to be operated on again, we found him at another acceptance level the second time around—higher in some cases, lower in others—and in each case the healing time differed correspondingly. But we had no means of determining objectively and systematically what had happened in the patient's life during the interval, and so we cannot say for certain what factors were at work.

We do have some fairly good ideas. In the two cases I mentioned at the beginning, both patients seemed to be bottled up in negative feelings which had them saying "no" to their experience. When the feelings were released in the course of pastoral counseling, the patients found they could say "yes," and they healed. In other cases, changes in acceptance level appeared to accompany episodes of pastoral counseling, prayer, or the administration of sacraments. But these changes were not subjected to controlled study, and thus we cannot at this point claim that there is any correlation between pastoral care and speed of healing. My caution here is overwhelming, as you can perhaps appreciate, because I would not be in the chaplaincy if I did not believe that pastoral care could speed up healing. It will not be long, I think, before we can demonstrate the correlation in responsible research.

Dysfunctional Dualism

What, then, are the implications of this study for our concern with healing and salvation? In the division of labor among the helping professions, we commonly separate the tasks of healing and salvation as two distinct concerns. Medicine takes care of healing and religion looks after salvation. As a practical matter, it is probably well that we stick to this division. Either task is enough to command the whole of a person's life, and the differences in basic knowledge, training, vocabulary, and working methods are so great as to make it unlikely that any one person will be able to encompass both with any degree of excellence. I doubt if it helps much for a surgeon to pray with a patient before an operation, any more than it would help for a clergyman to try to assist at the operating table. A functional dualism here makes sense.

But when we move from the practical matter of how we best function to the consideration of what healing and salvation are about—what they mean in terms of total well-being and the concepts on which they are based—such a dualism tends to defeat the efforts of both medicine and religion. If we permit the differentiation of our functions to imply a dichotomy in man between body and soul, we are playing human nature false and probably are doing violence to the people we try to help. Dichotomized, man finds neither healing nor salvation.

That, historically, is what the Western world has done—it split man in two. This process within Christianity began in the latter part of the first century at Alexandria and Antioch with the revival of Plato's doctrine of forms and the elaboration of the distinction between substance and essence to apply to the nature of man. Biblical religion prior to that time saw man as a unitary whole, one with all creation, and used interchangeably the words *nephesh, ruach, beten, basar* in the Hebrew and *psyche, pneuma, soma, sarx* in the Greek to denote man in his wholeness as a creature. But the church fathers of the second century, yielding to neoplatonic dualism, set these terms in opposition.

Nephesh and *psyche,* which later in English came to be translated as "soul," and *ruach* and *pneuma,* which came to be translated as "spirit," were set off in opposition to *beten* and *soma,* which became "body," and *basar* and *sarx,* which became "flesh." Between soul and body, between spirit and flesh, a line was drawn. Soul and spirit were placed above the line, body and flesh below. From that time on, the Western world regarded man as a dual being, possessed of a higher nature comprising his powers of reason, will, and aspiration—his spirituality; and a lower nature, comprising his emotions, appetites, and bodily functions—his bestiality. Today this view is known as Cartesian dualism, but Descartes merely restated what the Western world had believed for centuries.

Some of the consequences of this view have been disastrous. In Christendom it has produced an angelistic concept of human nature which has made us ashamed and apologetic for the human body, dishonest about our emotions, unable to accept ourselves as creatures. The recent papal encyclical on birth control is a final reduction to absurdity of this angelistic view of human nature. It so divorces man's spiritual pretension from biological reality as to make a mockery of biblical religion. This is the ultimate heresy: that man be required to deny his flesh and behave as if he were an angel.

This notion that man is a spiritual being, of a higher order than all the rest of creation, while it has stimulated many of the advances of civilization, has also led us to an arrogant exploitation of nature which has so upset the ecological balance as to threaten our survival. Man is proliferating like a cancer on the earth, devouring everything in his path; he is in danger now of devouring himself.

A more immediate consequence, for those of us who are concerned with the day-to-day problems of patient care, is the extent to which this dualistic view of human nature has carried us beyond a practical division of labor in the work of healing and salvation to a conceptual divorce between the two concerns. We see no real relationship between the two, and we pursue our own concern in disregard of the other. The doctor treats the body and the clergyman the soul, and never the twain shall meet.

Although we talk a great deal about "total patient care," in actuality we show little evidence of believing in it. We seem quite content to deal with a patient as if the only thing that mattered was the welfare of his body, if we are doctors, or of his spirit, if we are clergy. We do, of course, tip our hats to each other as a gesture of courtesy, and sentimentalize about the importance of both the body and the soul—and then go right on as we were before, preoccupied either with laboratory findings, the mechanics of surgery, and stomping out disease or with the rituals of religion, pious reassurance, bombarding God with prayer. The trouble is we are stomping on human beings in the process. The bombardment backfires. We sometimes wind up with sicker patients than we had before, neither healed nor saved.

Salvation and Health: Wholeness

If this study implies one thing, it is that the human being is all of one piece, and we cannot differentiate his physical and spiritual attributes as if they stood for separate entities to be treated independently. Either we treat him in his wholeness as a human being or we do not really treat him at all. Both physician and clergyman must constantly ask: What is this patient as a person saying about life? What message does he convey through his body signs or through his attitudes and aspirations? For these are both expressions of a single reality, the person's total response to whatever threatens his well-being. Both are expressions of the person.

The biblical words for healing and salvation have the same root meaning in both the Hebrew and the Greek. The meaning is ultimately *to be made whole*. The distinction we have made between them, under the influence of the neoplatonic dualism, applying healing to the body and salvation to the soul, is utterly alien to the Bible. Man's health is his salvation, and his salvation is his health; for both are signs of his wholeness as a creature.

A great deal of evidence is available from research in many different fields to demonstrate the continuity of all aspects of man's being. Simply to indicate the relevant studies would require another chapter. It seems at this stage as if the best way to describe man's nature is to describe it as an energy-transfer system which ranges all the way from DNA to mystical experience over one unbroken continuum. We can call this "mechanistic" or "materialistic" if we choose, but those words have meaning only in a dualistic frame of reference. Get rid of dualism; give up once and for all the notions of body and soul; attend to the behavior of the live human being in his totality; learn again to cherish him as creature; and we may begin to save man from the damnation of a false spirituality, and recover that ancient health which is salvation.

12
Peeling the Healing Onion

BY LOWELL H. MAYS

For a moment let us consider a variation on an old theme. Once upon a time there was a fellow who was traveling from Jerusalem to Jericho, and en route he fell among some rough people who chose to mug him and rob him of his goods. We can assess his condition as a simple manifestation of the predicament of man.

The drama begins to take on a little color as actors express their roles. Enter on the scene, first, the primary agent of care. Whether he be a paramedic, a first-aid man, or a primary physician, we see the immediate requirements of the fellow who fell among rough guys being attended to. His wounds are nursed, his needs are addressed, and he seems to be in good hands. Enter, second, someone who begins criticizing the kind of care the individual is receiving, saying, "I indeed affirm everything that has been done thus far, but it is not enough." The second actor says that while he wants to support the role of the primary agent of healing and care, he would prefer to put his emphasis in seeing to it that this individual is transported from the early scene to a more capable and extensive kind of care. The second individual we might recognize as the modern ambulance driver or mobilized medic.

It does not seem at this point that the first two agents are in conflict. Each of them has a valid role, and each supports the other. The primary healing agent is not criticizing the mobilization officer, and the mobilization officer is not asking the primary agent to discontinue his effort. Enter party number three; he indicates that while he supports the first two actors and their effort, he really feels as though the traveler is going to require longer-term care, and he opens up an inn (or a hospital or an institution of mercy, if you like those terms better). The third individual does not criticize the first two: in fact, he applauds their efforts by saying that the man might not have been able to receive the advantages of his tertiary-care institution if it were not for good primary care and for someone being available to transport him from the scene of his trauma to longer-term facilities. The third actor, however, is very clearly stating that where he wishes to put his emphasis is on an institution with greater capabilities which may more appropriately care for the individual's needs. This facility may be able to diagnose more accurately and treat so that sound regeneration can be expected. It leans on technological advances such as intubation and intravenous feeding as well as on its diagnostic mechanisms of x-ray, blood tests, and various monitoring devices. Again, no one seems to be asking that anyone else be eliminated; in fact, all seem to be supporting one another.

At this point some would say we are now leaving the health care positions and going to other individuals. I would suggest that we need *not* leave the health care professions; in fact, it is my thesis that the health care professions should also be involved with the next levels of healing.

The fourth actor who appears on the scene is running around with a pad and pencil. He says that he has seen many people brought in from this road between Jerusalem and Jericho and indicates that it is a well-known fact that the road is rough and that there are lots of violent types living in the area. Therefore, he is getting up a petition to put in mercury vapor lights so that the entire area will be better lighted and the possibility of mugging will be reduced. Again, it does not seem as though anybody is trying to disqualify anyone else. It seems only that the level of concern is moving beyond where it has previously been recognized as a responsibility of the health care profession.

Enter the next actor. We might call him Archie Bunker, M.D., who represents the concern for law and order. He indicates to everyone that the problem might be more readily solved if we would fully admit that the road from Jerusalem to Jericho is going to be a rough road whether it is lighted or not. He signs the petition to get better lights but he also has his own petition to take to the common council to encourage them to put more police in the area and possibly patrol with dogs on a twenty-four-hour basis. Again, no one seems to be eliminating anyone, but rather the whole approach is becoming more diffuse. It would seem only logical that such broadening of concerns would be generally applauded. People are beginning to take pride in the fact that individuals have become concerned and have exerted some effort to stamp out these social problems and allow their professional capabilities to flank and support any endeavor to better manage them.

Enter a final actor. This individual begins by making a statement saying that he supports fully the efforts of all the previous individuals and hopes that those who have interest in these areas will join forces with the original spokesmen. He, however, says that he does not wish to put his time and effort in any of these areas of concern but rather wants to put all his clout at still another level. He asks the question: "What makes the muggers mug—that is, what kinds of environments do they come from that make them go out and be forced to thieve and rob and hurt people in order to function adequately?" This individual is asking a social-policy question: Why is it that individuals act the way they do? Is it because they are so utterly deprived in their background that they have to take things from someone else and make life for someone else difficult in order to be able to get the basic things they desire? Or is it possible that they wish to strike back at society because of the way they feel society treats them? That is, they may not need the things they steal, but their general social condition reinforces strong-arm tactics and they seem to get reward and their identity from being "strong" and aggressive. Another possibility might be that they have become so disappointed with their culture, or have such a malignant view of it, that they consider this to be almost the norm for human action. In this last layer of interest one might find that a theological treatise on the nature of man would be appropriate as a basic consideration in trying to find a remedy for the human predicament.

By having gone through this rather lengthy paraphrase of the parable of the good Samaritan, we can see where the traditional roles of health care are accentuated as well as expanded. When the original storyteller, Jesus, finishes the story he makes his point by asking a question and then by answering it with an imperative. He asks the question as to which one of three individuals who encountered the stricken man showed himself to be the neighbor of the afflicted. The response comes with the words that the neighbor was the one who showed mercy. Jesus then responds by saying, "Go, and do thou likewise (Luke 10:37)"—in other words, go and show mercy. It seems as though our current society is still being implored to show mercy.

The question as to how mercy is shown may indeed have become a stratified and complicated series of possibilities, but the imperative itself has never been removed. It certainly is merciful to bind up another's wounds; it is merciful to see that the individual is transported from the scene of the trauma to an institution providing more sophisticated care; it is merciful to work in such an institution; it is merciful to act in areas of prevention, such as better lighting and law enforcement; it is merciful to ask basic human questions as to why individuals behave the way they do; it is also merciful to put emphasis at any of these levels.

When Gordon Allport wrote the book *Becoming*,[1] he used the illustration of an onion, which grows from its center outward and adds dimensions to its existence as it continues to grow. He indicated that each dimension can be looked at separately, but that the onion makes more sense as a whole. Health care people are recognizing more fully the many different layers of professional care provided by other disciplines. For years lip service was given to other approaches such as those of occupational therapy, physical therapy, the behavioral sciences, and religion, but at the same time medical people seldom *acted* very sympathetically. On the contrary, it seemed as though they often pushed others arrogantly out of the way in order to do medicine's thing. As soon as they chose that posture, a familiar fact would be voiced —60 percent of the presentations made by outpatients did not exhibit real primary pathology which medicine could or should handle but rather lay in an area of mind or spirit which medicine was not equipped to treat. As the healing profession is looked at layer by layer—as the healing onion is peeled—we have to ask the question again: "What is the most appropriate way of showing mercy to individuals in our culture?" Or, more specifically, "What is the most effective thing for *you* to do, in order to show mercy?" It may not be your thing to be a primary healing agent or an ambulance driver, or to be at the institutional level, or to get up a petition, but somewhere you must find that which is your merciful encounter.

Altogether too often, medicine has not moved beyond the first, second, and third levels. Today medicine is receiving an invitation to get to the final level and assist in asking some of the basic questions concerning life.

The late theologian Paul Tillich has said, "In order to understand the nature of disease, one must know the essential nature of man as well as the possible distortion of it."[2]

For too long a time theology has allowed medicine to live with the impression that man now and then "gets sick," while theology should have been consistently helping medicine to understand that man is sick and that his sickness occasionally requires outpatient management and sometimes institutionalization in order to cope with the momentary manifestations of his sickness.

Until the healing profession recognizes that man is sick and that his very nature is one which needs regeneration, medical management will only be a continued frustration at the early levels of the encounter of that sickness.

Healing then, as Tillich suggests, is more than the removal of a diseased organ or the synthesizing of a chemical harmony in a living organism. In another work, Tillich says,

> Health is not the lack of divergent trends in our bodily or mental or spiritual life, but the power to keep them united. And healing is the act of reuniting them after the disruption of their unity. "Heal the sick" means—help them to regain their lost unity without depriving them of their abundance, without throwing them into a poverty of life perhaps by their own consent.[3]

When Christ points his disciples to the task of healing the sick and casting out demons, one can see by looking at Tillich's definition where this kind of mandate becomes reasonable and very necessary. When one looks at our society it is easily determined where the various levels of healing the sick can be located, such as in the numerous policy-forming places, and the concept of casting out demons becomes more understandable when you can begin to recognize the principalities and powers one must overcome in order to "Go, and do thou likewise" in this culture. Some of those demons may be government and tradition. It would seem that in order for a working relationship to be established between theology and medicine one might say to the two disciplines that it is high time they take each other seriously and link forces. It is futile for theologians to say to medical men that their forces should be linked: they have been saying it for years and haven't really accomplished much. Therefore, someone should say to the medical profession that they ought to look to the churches and other groups that recognize man's nature, wrestle with it, treat it, and celebrate the redemption of it. All of this probably could be said in more esoteric terms by stating that medicine should link forces with groups that heal man's nature rather than simply diagnose and treat it.

Many examples of such an interface might be cited. Dr. Granger E. Westberg, a noted theologian and one who has worked for many years within a medical context, has been saying that the crises in the health-care delivery in our country may be somewhat resolved in ghettos and in frontier situations by allowing local churches to be considered by the medical community as outpatient (or if need be, in some cases, inpatient) clinics. He has said that in many people's lives the church is already seen as a "clinic" or a place of healing, and that it will take a professional response of medicine for the society to be able to capitalize on that vision. Dr. Westberg was instrumental in seeing that such a clinic was established in Springfield, Ohio, and it is alive and well. Dr. Marc Hansen, professor of pediatrics at the University of Wisconsin Center for Health Sciences, applauded this concept and, while serving on the Governor's Task Force in Wisconsin, encouraged consideration of many similar kinds of health-care delivery.

Another model of the cooperation of such groups is the accommodation on some multi-specialty staffs of a representative of a behavioral discipline based in theology. A theologian based in behavioral understanding and concerned for healing, working within a medical model, has proved to be a significant member of the healing team at the University Health Service at the University of Wisconsin in Madison. This is an assignment that I assumed in July of 1972. Twenty-six physicians on the staff make referrals, and in this position I am asked to assist with patients in emotional distress. Value-system conflicts, marital adjustment, identity crises, and situational and reactional depressions are some of the kinds of problems which regularly are brought into my office. Consistent charting is maintained and a very interesting interchange has taken place between the discipline of medicine and the discipline of theology. The credit for such vision must be given to the director of the Health Service, Dr. J. D. Kabler, professor of medicine at the University of Wisconsin Center for Health Sciences.

Clinics throughout America are beginning to receive clergy on their staffs. One such clinic near Minneapolis already has two on a staff of a dozen physicians. These clergy maintain a consulting practice and send bills just like other specialists.

There must be developed a reformed understanding of what the Old Testament has always known as "the priest." The concept of priest eventually accommodates the role of healer and in the New Testament was seen as the local health officer. At any rate, he was concerned for the total health of the individual and the community. If, in order to treat a man, we must continually chop him into segments and put him in cubbyholes, we will find that he will constantly "get sick" and will not be viewed as "being sick"; he will be able to manipulate the system so as to avoid serious confrontation with his basic illnesses, and he may continually be frustrated and frustrate those who try to care for him. We have all heard practitioners say, "I know what has to be done, but I just can't seem to get through to the patient." This does not presume that a person working from a theological background will be able to reach every patient, but it does say that that person will have a different orientation and the patient may recognize the difference. Such a development of an interrelationship between theology and medicine will also call for opportunities of educating professionals in "ministry" together.

The physician ministers to the sick. The clergyman ministers to the sick. It would seem wise to educate both "ministers" in a common educational experience. Since 1970, I have been on the faculty of the University of Wisconsin Medical School trying to form at the place of medical education a "new" professional who may understand something about theology, ethics, and the human nature of man. Other medical schools throughout the country have also accepted theologians on their faculties. E. A. Vastyan, a priest of the Episcopal Church, is at the University of Pennsylvania at Hershey, and Sam Banks, a Baptist clergyman, is at the University of Florida in Gainesville; Roman Catholics like Father Richard McCormick at Georgetown could be cited. In some places where there are both medical and divinity schools there are joint appointments, such as Arthur

Dyck at Harvard and David Duncombe at Yale, whose main appointments are in the divinity school but who are also on the faculty of the school of medicine.

For years theological students have taken clinical training in various medical institutions. Now some medically trained professionals have been accepted on theological faculties. Wartburg Theological Seminary in Dubuque, Iowa, recently received a full-time psychiatrist on its faculty, for the purpose of teaching theology, not treating students.

Residences should be established for those wishing to work in the area of theology and medicine if this interface is to grow. The Kennedy Foundation has established fellowships for those wishing to work in ethics and medicine, but ethics is, of course, not the whole picture of theology.

Finally, both professions, theology and medicine, must allocate members of their profession to work together and to be present at all levels of concern in the social order. Theologians, moralists, medical people, and other individuals concerned for healing the total man will be wise to designate individuals to conjoin efforts at levels of policy-making decisions within the social order and to see that the layers of the healing onion are exposed. We have moved from the day of seeing physicians only in roles of bureaucrats within government to days of seeing physicians significantly involved in being politicians in government. The governor of the state of Wisconsin recently appointed a physician to be secretary of the Health Policy Council; Dr. James Kimmey sees his role to be that of a politician for the purpose of forming policies and then trying to get them through structures of government. It would be good if a theologian could be appointed to assist in shaping those policies and to guarantee that concern for the whole man will be visible at that high level of policy formation.

Many of these things suggest a giant step from the traditional categories where we have seen theology and medicine relate. No one is ever going to say that the bedside manner, the soothing concern, or the relevance of the supernatural is to be downplayed; however, it is necessary now to deploy theologians and medical men at all levels and to see that they are at those levels together. Only when there can be a conjunction of groups concerned for the total well-being of man can we expect man to become totally well.

13

Spiritual Healing

BY THE RT. REV. ALLEN W. BROWN, D.D., BISHOP OF ALBANY

It is evident to all men reading holy scripture and the ancient authors[1] that Spiritual Healing has been part of the practice of the church from its beginning. Its use was normal in the earlier days of the undivided church. At a later date the Healing Sacrament (Unction or the Laying On of Hands in healing) became, when practiced in the Western church, "Last Rites" with the emphasis on preparation for death rather than recovery. The rise of Lourdes as a healing cult (1859), the publication of Mary Baker Eddy's *Science and Health* (1875), of Percy Dearmer's *Body and Soul* (1909), and the healings of an English layman, M. Hickson, contributed to the revival of interest in the present century.

The New Testament accepts Spiritual Healing as normal in the everyday life of the church. A substantial part of the gospel narrative is concerned with the healing ministry of Christ himself, more than twenty such healing incidents being recorded. It should be noted that Christ worked no "miracles"[2] to call attention to himself; that issue was settled in the second temptation (Matthew 4:5-7); compassion unfailingly was the motive; faith on the part of the person healed, his friends, or family the prerequisite.[3] A direction to heal was part of Christ's commission; the authority was not limited to the ordained and was exercised by the Seventy, and perhaps by others, as well as by the Twelve and their successors, including Paul.

While the primary concern of the early Christian community was to proclaim the good news of the kingdom and to witness to the resurrection, it continued the healing ministry instituted by Christ himself. One notes, however, an abruptness about apostolic healings, almost as if compassion no longer were relevant and faith necessary only on the part of the minister of healing. Does this mark a subconscious beginning of clerical professionalism, a producer-consumer relationship, or is it only a difference in literary style? Generally, post-Pentecost healings were accomplished by the apostles or others working in pairs, who used the laying on of hands and anointing with oil which had been authorized by Christ (Mark 6:13; the classic reference, of course, is James 5:14) and also fasting. There is one example of objects, related to an apostle, possessing healing power (Acts 19:12—a beginning of the use of relics?). Peter's shadow also was believed to be therapeutic (Acts 5:15), but a man's shadow was regarded by the ancients as an extension of a man and not something having independent existence.

The Holy Spirit was at work in the New Testament church; the crippled and demon-possessed were cured, sins were forgiven, and the name of Jesus Christ of Nazareth was seen to possess healing power.

Thus first-generation Christians responded to their Lord, who initially had called twelve and later others "that they should be with him"[4] and that he might send them forth to preach and to have power to heal sickness and to cast out devils and who later said to the Twelve, and presumably to their successors, "As my Father hath sent me, even so send I you (John 20:21)."

The church continued to exercise an effective healing ministry until the fourth century.[5] Whether a failure to continue this ministry led to a loss of charismatic power or whether establishment led to an abandonment of this ministry is debatable. We do know that after Constantine, in a general way, healing no longer was part of the normal ministry of the church; the laying on of hands and anointing with oil were reduced to vestigial remains of earlier practice and survived as terminal rites. Only in recent times has the church begun to recapture an awareness of its healing power.

There seems to have been a greater acceptance of Spiritual Healing in the British Isles than in the United States. The (American) Episcopal Church, however, adopted an official Rite for the Anointing with Oil and the Laying On of Hands in 1928, the emphasis being on healing, and its General Convention in 1964 approved a lengthy and sympathetic report[6] prepared by a commission composed of informed medical persons, clergy, and laymen. The report, among other things, indicated that at that time at least five hundred parishes scheduled regular healing services. The Emmanuel Movement in Boston (1906), The Order of St. Luke the Beloved Physician, ecumenical in nature, the International Guild of St. Raphael (1915), the Academy of Religion and Mental Health, Lourdes, Saint Anne de Beaupré, and the work of such persons as Alice Gardner Neal, John Ellis Large,[7] and many others[8] have stimulated Spiritual Healing in the present century.

Spiritual Healing is not easily defined; the secularist probably will spell "Spiritual" with a small "s" and will define it as a form of therapy based on the interaction of mind and body, including the ability of the human mind to affect the well-being of the human body. It will be seen that, at the least, this is little more than autosuggestion; at its best, however, it recognizes the tremendous advances made by the mental sciences and is viable as far as it goes. It reminds older readers of Dr. Emile Coué's "Every day, and in every way, I am becoming better and better" and, while he would go far beyond the limits of this definition, of Norman Vincent Peale's "power of positive thinking."

The person concerned with Spiritual Healing will not ignore new insights of psychiatry and psychology; he will remember that, as discoveries in anatomy did not destroy the integrity of the body, so new insights into how personality functions do not negate personhood.

The theist, while not denying the importance of right thinking and the power of autosuggestion, insists that another factor is involved, the healing power of God. The late John Hayes Holmes, a theistic Unitarian, came to accept the principle of a para-natural[9] therapeutic Power, as do most independent healing cults and the Jewish Healing Science, a more or less non-Christian equivalent of Christian Science.

The Christian who believes in Spiritual Healing may feel that Spiritual is too ethereal a word and consider the term faith healing preferable (some Spiritual Healing literature seems to deemphasize physical cure). The believing Christian will assert that all healing (chemical, biological, surgical, and spiritual) is of God. He will recognize that the church's healing ministry derives from the ministry of Christ, is not restricted to the ordained,[10] and is eschatological in that it is a pledge of wholeness in the world to come. He also will assert that God the Holy Spirit is the acting agent in the healing process. The Christian, then, loosely defines Spiritual Healing as "a form of therapy which recognizes the availability of specific healing power, derived from the ministry of Christ, and made effective by the action of the Holy Spirit."

The third quarter of the twentieth century produced a theological climate hostile to any concept of Spiritual Healing other than as autosuggestion. This rise of a secular mind-set within the believing community is a matter of record. Authority became relative, the gospel a myth, and God was proclaimed by his theologians to be dead. A theologian without God is something of a contradiction in terms! Eventually thoughtful persons began to discover that the denial of God leads ultimately to the denial of man.

While the existence of God no longer is the issue, other problems remain. Contemporary man has mixed feelings about anything suggesting magic,[11] and the laying on of hands looks suspiciously like the "King's Touch" as practiced as late as 1709. Magic implies that the right person, the right action, the right words will produce an incalculable result. Spiritual Healing is the action of a loving God. The possibility of coincidence is not to be ignored; there is no clear-cut statistical evidence; successes and failures seem to come out about even, and death itself remains!

Holy scripture does not attribute almightiness to God in the present order, and medical science is aware of its limitations. Unanswered prayer, medical failure, and the fact of physical death will not preclude the exercise of every available healing power. Prudence will not allow the man of faith to do otherwise. Evidence for the validity of Spiritual Healing rests upon specific cases and upon the premise that back of the universe there is a loving God.

The phenomenon of nonmedical healing admits, as we have seen, a variety of definitions and is not strictly a Christian thing. The Christian, however, believes the Holy Spirit to be at work in all of life and is prepared to accept such a specific ministry without too rigid a definition[12] and without denying the validity of other healings, whether psychic, surgical, or chemical.

It has been the author's privilege to share in some extension of Christ's healing ministry. This experience leads to certain conclusions:

1. There is such a phenomenon as Spiritual Healing.

2. Because "spiritual" and "medical" healing are complementary, medical healing is more effective when reinforced by Spiritual Healing; the medical profession ought to give more attention to the phenomenon.

3. Because "spiritual" and "medical" healing are complementary, Spiritual Healing ought to be practiced normally only in conjunction with medical (and/or psychiatric) care.[13]

4. The church, as a special vehicle of the Holy Spirit, is under moral and pastoral obligation to study and to exercise its healing ministry.

14

Hale and Hearty

BY RABBI DAVID B. ALPERT

Sickness involves a trial of the spirit and is truly a spiritual experience. Much that occurs in illness is nonmedical, nonphysiological. What happens to the patient and what goes on in his mind are aspects of his illness.

Sickness compels reflection upon the nature and course of life and often represents the first real opportunity for a person to confront his inner questions. However worded, the essence and meaning of the self-examination is theological and religious in nature. What am I doing with my life? What am I here for, not alone in the hospital, but also upon this earth? What do I expect from life? What is the human being? What is life, and where did I go wrong, and why this punishment? These are among the questions sick people have, and they reach beyond medical and physiological areas.

Is punishment a causative factor? Break the law, and you may be punished. Violate the rules of good health, and you may suffer. Scrupulously observe the laws, and there may still be pain and suffering. Observe all the moral laws carefully, and you may still be the innocent victim. The sickness may be milder, or you may be able to see it as "the chastisements of love" and to accept it with better spirit. Punishment is not the sole causative factor in illness; no theory of retribution and the punitive explains all sickness. We must reject the idea that all sickness is due to punishment alone.

Involved is our concept of God and of the universe. To see the universe as vindictive, and to believe that God is merely punitive in nature, noting every peccadillo and "getting even" with every offender, is to dishonor and to misunderstand religion.

Another persistent and erroneous explanation that must be rejected is that of the malediction as the principal causative factor in illness. Many patients torment themselves in searching their memories for unkind words spoken to or about them in the distant past, a "hex" or curse that was spoken many years previously and returns after many years to induce the sickness. There is no evidence for any such thing. Nor does it help the patient to attribute his malady to bitter words and to unkind speech.

To relieve pain is a noble ideal. In every kind of hospital, sick people are used to pain, have learned to bear it or to find relief from it with the help of physicians and medications. But what can we do about the painful? The questions about the cause of their illness are one aspect of the painful in the experience of the sick. It is painful to acknowledge that some pet theories do not hold up, that tenaciously held ideas or explanations must be abandoned and unlearned, that we are not as strong as we think, that different interpretations and ideas must be learned or adopted. Sickness compels an examination of one's faith and beliefs—of pondering anew words that one has hitherto repeated without much thought. "The wrath of God" and "the vengeance of God" suggest hazy notions but are to be rejected as without foundation or curative value. The jingle goes, "If you have faith, you have no problems. If you have no faith, there are no solutions."

Among ideas that should be reexamined and rejected is the literal interpretation of "enemy" in the book of Psalms. Who is the enemy so often mentioned in Psalms, or with equivalent words of reference? It is the discordant, the disharmonious, the dis-ease in life. The enemy is not an actual malefactor, a person we can identify. The enemy is the inimical, the unfriendly, the hostile and unexplained life circumstances. A survey of the psalms, taking passages out of context, will illustrate that they speak of the painful. The quotations are taken from the *King James Version*, as the most familiar text.

"Thou preparest a table before me in the presence of mine enemies (Ps. 23:5)." In the lyric pastoral scenes of tender beauty, the sudden introduction of the enemy refers not to a person but to the doubts and puzzling circumstances which the person faces: Sickness and trouble and adversity are part-time enemies! Instead of "the valley of the shadow of death," the reading should be "the valley . . . of gloom and doubt." No book is used more in the sickroom than the Psalms, for the comfort and courage it offers to the discouraged, for the description of the feelings and emotions of sick people.

A theological element is unfortunately introduced in the *King James* English of Psalm 1, in the word ungodly for the simple Hebrew word *rasha,* meaning evil person. The sick person thus tends to identify with the "ungodly" who has been negligent of pious duties or careless in church attendance. The review of one's life (such as sickness can induce) produces painful queries, such as "What were my opportunities and what were my limitations, and could I have overcome those limitations?"

"Lord, how are they increased that trouble me. . . . I will not be afraid of ten thousands of people that have set themselves against me. . . . Thou hast smitten all my enemies." These lines from Psalm 3 may suggest the paranoid who actually fears that many people are out to get him as persecutors and agents of malice. But here again the word enemy is not to be taken literally as an injurer. Instead, enemy and the equivalent words "they . . . that trouble me" represent the musings of a person's mind and the tasks and responsibilities that he faces—and that he exaggerates to himself. An ancient commentary said that David saw himself as the enemy—thinking of his own needs and how to meet them. (In a sense, is not every one his own worst enemy?)

The enemy in Psalms holds the key to the understanding of the Psalter and deals with every emotion and turmoil that we have come to know among the sick. Instead of seeking incidents in the life of King David to regard as the situation which gave birth to the expression, we look to the psalms for experiences and circumstances familiar in the sickroom, even in verbalizing emotions that we still find. The first-person "I" who speaks in Psalms may be the universal heartbeat of mankind, the experience of everyone who identifies with the emotions and who is confronted with the similar sense of the painful, of the inimical, as he reviews life and would plan.

"Thou hast enlarged me when I was in distress" in Psalm 4 reminds us that the same root in Hebrew gives words that mean enemy, narrow, or trouble or distress; and that here the translation "distress" is perfectly proper and need not refer to a person as injurer but to the uncertainties. Every patient finds it painful to wonder, "Will my infirmity spread so that I shall become helpless, and of no use, and entirely dependent upon others?" Our unreasoning hope, as Americans, is that we shall continue to be able to function independently, that we shall not be a burden upon others or dependent upon them, and that we shall enjoy the fullest freedom of movement.

"Lead me, O Lord, in thy righteousness because of mine enemies," in Psalm 5, continues, "for . . . their inward part is very wickedness; their throat is an open sepulchre." The scholars point out the similarity of the words for grave or sepulchre—and for inward parts. Thus the enemy is torture of mind, the inner unrest and disquiet, the emotional stress, of that which unnerves a person. The enemy is the vague sense of attrition, the undefined problems.

"Mine eye is consumed because of grief; it waxeth old because of all mine enemies (Ps. 6:7)" reminds us of what is often heard in the hospitals. The enemies are not actual molesters but rather the vague uncertainties and the sense of the painful which trouble the sick. Of course, the psalms were not written with special reference to the sick person alone. But in them we find the record of the inner feelings and emotions of the sick person, and thus they often clarify what we experience among the sick.

"Depart from me, all ye workers of iniquity (Ps. 6:8)" need not refer specifically to identified people. May not the workers of iniquity be the system and the rules within hospitals which make for all kinds of delays in getting an answer or even needed equipment or repairs?

"Out of the mouth of babes and sucklings hast thou ordained strength because of thine enemies, that thou mightest still the enemy and the avenger (Ps. 8:2)" brings to mind the questions asked so frequently from the sickbed—What is man? What is the human being?—with the inner hope that somehow man, with all his imperfections, is still little lower than the angels (really, than God). But the feeling also is that even babes and infants have a better sense of appreciation of the wonders and grandeur of the nature of the universe and of nature than do the rules and the systems by which hospitals are run. In the lovely picture of infants thrilled at the beauty of nature, we hear the reminder of the psalms as prayer in the sickroom.

"When mine enemies are turned back, they shall fall. . . . The Lord also will be a refuge for the oppressed, refuge in times of trouble. Have mercy upon me, O Lord; consider my trouble. . . ." Psalm 9 clearly deals with the painful. The enemies represent undefined troubles, oppressive circumstances, unfilled needs, unanswered doubts and uncertainties. "O Lord . . . why hidest thou thyself in times of trouble? The wicked in his pride . . . as for all his enemies, he puffeth at them." Psalm 10 also equates enemy with trouble.

"With flattering lips and with a double heart do they speak (Ps. 12:2)" may refer to the slander or unkind words that make a sick person feel accursed by words of malediction spoken long ago.

"Lest mine enemy say, I have prevailed against him" in Psalm 13 reminds one of the patient who says, "What is the score? Anyway, I believe in God, I trust in God, and I am going to beat this rap." Determination and willpower can subdue the enemy—again, not a particular person, but unfriendly circumstances and sickness.

"Thou hast proved mine heart; thou hast visited me in the night; thou hast tried me, and shalt find nothing (Ps. 17:3)" is reminiscent of the mood of the patient undergoing tests of all sorts. Proved and tried—they also mean being tested. Every person undergoing medical tests hopes, in elliptical speech, that the tests will turn up nothing—that there is nothing serious, that the report will be negative. What patient would not reassure himself that he speaks honestly, not out of "feigned lips"? He pleads, "Hold up my goings in thy paths. . . . Shew thy marvelous lovingkindness . . . keep me as the apple of the eye. . . . From the wicked that oppress me, from my deadly enemies . . . deliver my soul from the wicked." (See Psalm 17.) The enemies and the oppressions are the serious fears and apprehensions, the anxious concerns in the mind of the person, the painful which disturbs.

This interpretation suits the psalm much better than theories of black magic, superstition, pseudomysticism, or identification of the enemy with the irrational and the workers of witchcraft. The psalms were not written with the sickroom in mind; but it is today in the sickroom that we have the proper clinical conditions under which best to understand and to apply them.

Each of the psalms starts with the conviction that genuine prayers to God are heard and are answered. The answer may not seem the one we desire, but it can fortify us with courage for the next instant (if nothing more). God attends to sincere prayer. Often, however, the sick person himself is too tired or too weak to say his own prayers. Then he must rely heavily upon the kind thoughtfulness of friends and well-wishers to pray for him and on his behalf. "Thy faith hath made thee whole (Matt. 9:22)." Faith healing can be documented, though the Psalter has no direct suggestion of faith healing or miraculous cure. In truth every recovery is itself a miracle, not to be explained by ordinary means.

To cast out devils, or to exorcise unclean spirits, to demonstrate healing miracles, suggests that it is necessary to get rid of the painful enemy in the mind of people to establish the proper conditions for healing. Healing and therapy have the same meaning originally. The word healing has become associated with the arts of healing; and the word therapy seems now to be confined to the science of medicine. Medicine is both art and science, and the art of healing is still essential.

"He delivered me from my strong enemy, and from them which hated me (Ps. 18:17)." This is not the foe in war, nor "the enemy" in current usage. To identify the sides in battle is no longer a simple matter; to indicate clearly the diagnosis and the prognosis of illness is hardly a simple matter either.

"Thine hand shall find out all thine enemies; thy right hand shall find out those that hate thee. . . . For they intended evil against thee; they imagined a mischievous device, which they are not able to perform (Ps. 21:8, 11)." A specific and definite person or persons, as the actual molester and enemy, may well be a passing thought. More likely the mind seeks to personify one's difficulties. To blame someone, real or imagined, is familiar. Yet the painful cannot be localized, nor the unpleasant circumstances tied to a person.

Is faith healing on a vast scale possible? Can a preacher before a large congregation of unknown people, have the ability to heal disease and to cure maladies and to remove pain from all in the congregation? Can a radio preacher, without seeing any of his listeners and without any power of individualization, extend his blessings? This seems unconvincing.

"For the king trusteth in the Lord. . . . Thine hand shall find out all thine enemies (Ps.21:8-9)." The executive officer of a big corporation almost resembles a king in his rule, with powers and authority and reputation for doing big things. For all his importance, something very tiny can send him to the hospital; a kidney stone, a very small vein or such, strips him of his glory. The enemy is something very small that reduces his ego and teaches him the wisdom of the body. "Thou preventest him with the blessings of goodness (Ps.21:3)" indicates a change in meaning of the word prevent. Not that the person will be stopped from receiving good; rather, the original meaning was that the goodness would come before him and would anticipate his needs.

"Be not far from me; for trouble is near; for there is none to help (Ps. 22:11)." The opening verse of this psalm is quoted in the New Testament and in the song "Eili Eili": "My God, my God, why hast thou forsaken me?" In this psalm, there is no mention of enemy. The word for trouble is cognate with the word for enemy. Instead, the psalmist uses many equivalent terms—worm, bulls, roaring lion, poured out like water—and such words are reminders that the concern is the painful, the overwhelming and impersonal circumstance.

Psalm 23 is pastoral and idyllic, with a sudden jarring note. "Thou preparest a table before me in the presence of mine enemies.... Surely goodness and mercy shall follow me (Ps. 23:5, 6)." The word follow is the same word used in other connections for enemies, or pursuers. The enemy and the pursuer are not to be identified as actual persons; they refer to the problems, the uncertainties, and even the troubling certainties.

"The troubles of my heart are enlarged.... Look upon mine affliction and my pain.... Consider mine enemies; for they are many (Ps. 25:17-19)." Whether the Hebrew word be *oyeb* or *sonay* or *zorrer*, often used interchangeably, it should be clear that the enemy is not a personal antagonist. The enemy is a comprehensive way of reference to the problems, the circumstances that puzzle and that seem beyond control, the discordant that accentuates trouble without necessarily being associated with a specific person. This truly represents the mood of many long-term sick people!

Examples of what sick people have found to be the painful and/or the enemy are frequent in the experience of the hospital chaplain. The painful often takes the form of questions that the patient asks himself even as he confides in the chaplain. What are my legitimate requirements and needs? Will I become entirely helpless and dependent on the mercy of others, or will I be able to help out on simple needs of my own? Will I lose my power of speech or power of movement? What is the human being, and how well have I fulfilled my qualities as a human being?

To relieve pain and to reduce suffering have been the working ideal of medicine. All of us are grateful for the tremendous and valiant services of the medical profession. Many quiet sufferers have learned to put up with and to seek help from pain when really necessary.

Every person with a lingering disease faces the painful (and the "enemy") with fear. There seems no help. What are some elements of the painful to be assuaged? To feel that one is likely to become helpless. The terrors of loneliness and rejection. To know that one is truly homeless. Unwelcome changes in personality. To sense that one has a limited future and a frozen past. Unable to meet one's needs and demands. To feel not wanted in a world of aggressive youth with whom it is difficult to compete. The necessity to detach oneself from things and friends. To wonder which doctor to trust, and in whom to place confidence. Fear of being a burden. Unable to take care of things or of self. Rejection and isolation. Unable to sense value in one's own life. Costs of illness. How to describe or mention illness when seeking employment. Relation to family. Whether to accept proposed treatment or not. Boredom and tiredness, and loss of interest even in TV or radio. To seem useless. Helpless and perhaps hopeless. These are some of the lesser forms of the "enemy"—painful.

The painful or the major enemies in illness are the religious and philosophical questions. What is life? And the human being? What is man? What is the soul? How justify the course of my life? What is God? And what really are my beliefs and feelings about God and the universe? Is death part of life? What is faith? What do I believe? What does my life add up to? Is the universe within comprehension and compassion? What are the purposes of life and how well have they been fulfilled? How does prayer help? Does the individual remain insignificant in the universe? What is the real me? Does God care? These are the painful questions with which the invalid struggles.

"A faithful friend is the medicine of life." "A cheerful heart is the best medicine." These axioms come from the book of Proverbs (17:17, 22).

Loneliness and actual homelessness. Why do these make me

feel more useless? Our society has made it a matter of pride to be independent and not to be a burden upon others. The judgment of the man on the street is that it is both disgraceful and dishonorable in any way to depend upon others, lest the picture of the self-made man be shattered. This notion has done considerable damage. In health, almost as much as in sickness, we are dependent upon many other people for many things. None of us is self-contained. The successful businessman is truly dependent upon many customers and faithful employees for the business to which he gave leadership and management. In the care of the sick it is especially necessary that we recognize our interdependence.

This would be one step in achieving the favorite slogan of recent days, the "dignity of the individual." Whatever we would respect as of highest worth and consideration, we would invest with dignity. This refers evidently to the inner inherent and real qualities of the person, to see him at his best, judged in the highest measure of merit and fulfilling the old religious idiom of "made in the image of God." The dignity of the person recognizes the essence and quality of the individual in whom we have come to recognize a human being, with unique human quality to the extent that we honor how he met adversity, how he responded to circumstance, how bravely he met pain and adversity, how bravely he bore suffering, and how well regarded his judgment was and is to be trusted.

"When the wicked, even mine enemies and my foes, came upon me to eat up my flesh, they stumbled and fell. Though an host should encamp against me, my heart shall not fear. . . . And now shall mine head be lifted up above mine enemies (Ps. 27:2-3, 6)." The construction of this psalm moves forward and backward in its thought process. The mind of the patient wavers between medical orders which go to the heart of the philosophic arguments on freedom versus determinism. In simple English, to the patient, the difference is between "You must" (usually "You must *not*") and the medical permission, "You may." "You must" carries with it the restrictions and the indications of severe illness: you must stay in bed, you must not have a telephone or visitors, you must not get out of bed, you must follow this regimen of medication—and the patient feels that every shred of freedom and of independence is taken from him. The sick person yearns for the relaxing of orders, the day when he will be told, "You may leave the bed, you may take a few steps, you may have the house diet." This means to the patient that his freedom as a person is restored, and that he is on the road to recovery. "You must" makes the patient feel under duress; "You may" fills the patient with eager desire to live and to use his new liberty.

That he notices others in the ward are much sicker than he, is often the strongest determinant for a patient to make every effort to "beat the rap" and to get well. He is inwardly encouraged by the feeling that he is not the most sick on the floor. He attunes his ears and eyes to what is going on in the room, on the floor; the sick are often asking and answering, "What is the score?"

"I will extol thee, O Lord; for thou hast lifted me up, and hast not made my foes to rejoice over me (Ps. 30:1)." The superscription mentions "the dedication of the house of the Lord." Nothing in the psalm suggests any direct connection with the Temple itself. But the recovery from serious illness, the assurance of the healing that comes with the help of God, represents to the individual something as momentous as the festivities at the dedication of a temple. "For his anger endureth but a moment; in his favor is life. . . . And in my prosperity I said, I shall never be moved (Ps. 30:5-6)." Pain (like anger) is intermittant and discontinuous. "I shall never be moved" suggests that one's footing will be secure, that one will not slip nor fall. The same phrase is used in Psalm 121.

"He will not suffer thy foot to be moved (Ps. 121:3)" can easily be misunderstood. By itself, this verse suggests that the person will stand completely immobilized, paralyzed, unable to move. The entire psalm needs another look. Psalm 121 can be of enormous benefit to patients if better understood. "I will lift up mine eyes unto the hills. From where cometh my help?" The second part of the opening verse is a question, which is not indicated in the *King James* translation. The response to the question is thus very emphatic. "My help cometh from the Lord. . . . He will not suffer thy foot to be moved: he that keepeth thee will not slumber." That is, you will be able to walk with full confidence, and without any fear of slipping or tripping or stumbling or falling. After surgery or temporary paralysis, a person loses the use of his legs and must very, very painfully learn to walk again. He is supported by the aluminum walker but is very apprehensive and fearful. Quoting this psalm to many people learning again to take their first few steps has been helpful in restoring their confidence. The physical therapist or nurse who accompanies the patient learning to walk acknowledges the help of this psalm addressed to the patient. "You will walk with confidence, without fear; your legs will support you and will not crumble under you; feel that your help still comes from God, that you may walk securely."

"Their idols are . . . the work of men's hands. They have mouths, but they speak not; eyes have they, but they see not. They have ears, but they hear not: noses have they, but they smell not. They have hands, but they handle not: feet have they, but they walk not: neither speak they through their throat (Ps. 115:4-7)." What we have here are accurate descriptions of people in chronic hospitals—people who have lost the power of speech, who have lost the power of sight or of movement, who have lost the power of walking. The suggestion would then be that idolatry is itself some form of illness. To seek to regain the power of speech, or the power of walking, seems very painful to the person involved—and proceeds very slowly.

A twelve-year-old girl recovered her power of walking, *Talitha cumi* in Mark being interpreted, "Damsel, I say unto thee, arise (Mark 5:41)." This account reminds us of a variant reading of Amos 5:2. The *King James* reads, "The virgin of Israel is fallen; she shall no more rise." The variant reading is, "She has fallen. No more to fall. Arise and walk, O virgin of Israel." This variant reading follows exactly the Hebrew word order and places the emphasis on the ability to walk, to recover the power of walking. These passages are of considerable value in talking to patients temporarily deprived of the power to walk.

To the highly intelligent, speech loss or speech that becomes heavy is something very painful. The anxiety that illness will permanently deprive one of his power of speech, or walking, or sight is very painful.

Many phrases are retained in everyday speech because they are picturesque and not to be taken literally. We say that "we are spellbound by a play" or that "a movie fascinated us," yet actually we have not been under a continuing spell. In the Bible, the "enemy" is also a comprehensive picturesque phrase to indicate the discordant and the threatening experiences.

"I will be glad and rejoice in thy mercy: for thou hast considered my trouble; thou hast known my soul in adversities; And hast not shut me up into the hand of the enemy. . . . My times are in thy hand; deliver me from the hand of mine enemies and from them that persecute me (Ps. 31:7-8, 15)." In this psalm, enemy and troubles are used interchangeably, and the "enemy" is not clothed as an actual person easily recognized. Clearly the enemy is the painful that patients find vexing. A secondary theme in this particular psalm refers to "lying vanities" and "lying lips." This is a reminder again of the maledictions and unkind words of the past from which the patient feels he now suffers. Those were words that others had spoken.

On the other hand, many patients (as part of illness) manifest an unwitting power to say cutting things to their close family. The patient may say that he has no intention of hurting, though he speaks the words which get under the skin of his close relatives and upsets them. "Why do you keep me here, and when will you take me home, and are you inviting my death?" Something in the nature of long illness evokes such remarks from the patient, which make hospital visits more of a strain to the family.

In the most strict use of language, many people are in hospitals and nursing homes because they are homeless. The records have some sort of address for them as place of legal residence, but homeless is an accurate description for many in these institutions. They have no home to go to. They could not live alone. They were unwelcome in the family setting, and the family could not take care of them. To recognize that next-of-kin have no place for you only intensifies one's dread and loneliness. It is indeed painful to feel dependent upon the mercy of strangers, and to be unable to fend for oneself. Not to have a place you call home, or that you know will take you in under necessity, is part of the painful.

"Let not them that are mine enemies wrongfully rejoice over me: neither let them wink with the eye that hate me without a cause." Psalm 35 is a good example of the tossing back and forth in the mind of the sick as he appeals for the help of God.

The references to "enemies" and "them that hate me" are indistinct as people but clear as that which bothers and seems unmanageable.

We turn to the psalms to comfort the sick. But the psalms also help throw light and enable us to recognize some of the nonmedical elements of illness. Medicine can do wonders to relieve pain and to conquer many discomforts. Many disturbing thoughts run through the mind of the sick which seem unrelated to the illness. These fugitive thoughts are often of the painful: the dread of being helpless, of being lonely, of becoming increasingly dependent, of losing one's home, of becoming the victim of the harsh and vindictive words from others, even of losing one's dignity.

The dignity of the individual has the measure of the highest approval that we can convoke. The "dignity of the individual" has become a matter of sharp debate in connection with the care of the sick and dying.

A few years ago, tremendous pressure was put upon physicians with "money is no object. Do all you can to save the life of this person." That is rarely heard now. Instead, the families suggest to the physician, "Let this person not suffer. We hate to see him writhe and suffer." Thus, in the name of the dignity, the family now asks that medical treatment not be continued beyond a certain point, and the decision when medications shall be withheld is to be made by the family rather than the physician. Physicians have a great respect for life. Their judgment should be considered. Is the patient the best judge of his needs? Is the family the best judge of what is best for the sick person? The answer to both questions must be no. But there has been considerable criticism that members of the medical profession have been administering too much medicine and are too eager to apply last-minute drastic measures. The criticism has become so considerable that the families now ask for the right to decide when the point is reached that medication be withheld.

The family does this to spare the person undue suffering. But perhaps the real suffering is upon the family at the bedside.

15

The Role of Religion and Faith in Facing Physical and Mental Illness and Death

BY THE REV. GEORGE LEE GRAY

Christians believe that God is the Creator, the giver of life. We see God as the sustainer of life—the One who has created within each human body what can be called "healing qualities." The Bible speaks of Jesus' healing ministry in terms of a person who "was made whole." Both the physically ill and the emotionally ill and the emotionally disturbed were touched by the Master, and they "were made whole." In our life today we often see these healing qualities of our Master at work in mind and body.

To be a part of a great hospital, to be privileged daily to observe the dedicated work of physicians and surgeons, is a great satisfaction. These people are able to do great things, but the best and the greatest of the medical profession realize they work always within the bounds and limits of God's creative genius. The surgeon of today is able to perform brilliant operations—brain surgery, open heart surgery, lung surgery, kidney transplants—but his scalpel has no healing power. It cuts, wounds, opens the body, removes infected tissue and diseased and defective organs, and then the healing qualities which God has placed in that body have to take over and heal the surgeon's wound and restore the patient to health.

So it is with the physician. He uses many methods of diagnosis; he discovers a powerful germ deep within a body and uses a more powerful drug to curtail the power of the germ. But the drug does not heal the poisoned tissues. The God-given healing qualities are called forth and begin to restore health after the high-powered drug has conquered the germ.

In this mysterious act we behold the handiwork of God. We witness the cooperation of God and man in the healing of physical and mental illness. The healing of a cut finger is awesomely beautiful. To witness the recovery of a person who has suffered an emotional illness is a thrilling experience. These things cause a Christian to rejoice at the realization of God's love and mercy and compassion as it issues forth in the healing process. Though we often take the healing of our bodies for granted, we are forced to admit it is a work of God.

Then there are times when we hear about, or witness at first hand, a person who is healed in a miraculous way. He gives evidence of having been "touched by the Master," for he is healed, made whole. And it is a miracle—inexplainable by medical science. These so-called miracles are not readily accepted by everyone. Some people say, "Yes, I believe in miracle healing." Others answer, "No, miracle healing does not happen in our day." And there are those who say, "I have heard of these things, but I personally do not know."

There have always been those who were skeptical of miracles. Jesus had many outspoken critics who beheld his miracles and still did not believe. And some of these skeptics are still around.

There is no doubt in my mind that the God of miracles of Jesus' day is the same God I serve today. I believe he is able to perform miracles, but I do not know when or where or how he will choose to intervene in human lives in a miraculous way. I cannot know if he will choose to work a miracle in a given individual. Therefore, I never pray in a demanding way for healing in a human life. I always pray for God's will to be done and for submission to that will. Faith is the great weapon of a Christian. Faith in God enables a person to trust God in all things—health, sickness, or death.

In my ministry I have encountered a number of situations where God seemed to move in a mysterious way:

Mr. A was a married man in his fifties. He was a Christian, and he and his family were active in their church. He began to suffer from shortness of breath, was hospitalized, and his condition was diagnosed as lung cancer. His family and friends prayed that he might be healed if it was God's will. Cobalt treatment was started and the tumor began to shrink and soon disappeared. Several years have passed and the tumor has not reappeared. This man, a man of great faith, believes his healing was a miracle, an act of God!

Mr. B was not a Christian, but his wife and children were. He suffered a stroke and was partially paralyzed for a while. His family and their Christian friends prayed. He improved steadily and was able to go home. After a period of time he returned to his work. He attended church with his family and became a Christian. This man and his family give God credit for his healing; they consider it a miracle. Today, they are people of strong faith.

Mrs. C was married, in her middle fifties, the mother of four sons. She had some physical problems and went to the doctor for an examination. She and her husband were told she had cancer. She was hospitalized, but the diagnosis was that the tumor was inoperable. She was permitted to go home, and the treatment was continued on an outpatient basis. This family—husband, wife, four sons, and their families—were Christians. They prayed, Christian friends prayed, and special prayer services were held at several churches. The husband stated, "I prayed always for God's will to be done, but I never felt it was God's will for my wife to die now. As I prayed I felt the same as when I prayed for our four sons when they were in service. They were all in the midst of the fighting in World War II, but God took care of them—not a hair on their heads was harmed." Today, over twenty years later, this woman is still alive. The cancer disappeared. This man and wife and their sons feel very strongly that God intervened in their lives in a miraculous way. They believe in miracle healing. These people, along with many others who witnessed this event of healing, are not religious fanatics, but they are people of strong faith. They have witnessed the moving of God in their midst.

Faith makes a great difference in the way a person faces life. Life at its best is not easy; it is very demanding, and there is always the underlying fear of what tomorrow may bring. Tragedy, dread disease, crisis, a long, confining illness with loss of earning ability, sudden death—these things happen every day all around us, and we always wonder when one or more of these might suddenly become a part of our lives. This is the point where faith takes over. As a minister friend of mine said in the midst of a long illness, "If I can only remember that the same Lord who has been with me thus far will continue to walk with me down this long dark road." He was gathering his faith, strengthening his forces, bracing for the battle which was before him. Every Christian has to do this same thing, for every day will not be sunny and beautiful. The storm clouds will come in every life someday, somewhere, somehow. No one escapes.

When sickness comes our faith makes the difference. A broken leg, appendicitis, minor surgery, major surgery, long days and nights in the hospital, sometimes many miles from home—all these demand faith to stand up and move toward a better day. A husband and father hears the dreaded words, "I'm sorry, Mr. Smith, but you aren't going to be able to continue in this same type of work with your bad back." But this is all the patient knows; he's never done anything else; he's been on the same job eighteen years. He hopes he will wake up and learn that what he has just heard is only a bad dream. But he knows it isn't a dream; it's true. What do you do at a time like this? The Christian remembers his faith and turns to God. All his questions will most likely not be answered, but the Holy Spirit, whom Jesus called the "Great Comforter," makes known his presence. "Yea, though I walk through the valley of the shadow of death, I will fear no evil: for thou art with me; thy rod and thy staff they comfort me (Ps. 23:4)." Much of the fear and dread is removed in his presence. Faith calls forth help from on high. For the Christian this is very real, not just an emotional upheaval, but often it comes as a quiet realization of the presence of God in the midst of a real crisis in our lives. And in this presence we take a new look at the situation—it's still the same, the same circumstances, but God is there. He takes us by the hand, and as we walk on through the dark we have a new courage, a new outlook, a new assurance. When I was a boy I would go anywhere on the darkest night if my father held my hand in his. I felt he could take care of me no matter what happened. When the Christian places his hand in God's, when he feels the presence of the Holy Spirit, the Great Comforter, then he knows that he is not alone in this crisis and that, whenever or wherever it ends, God will still be with him. I've watched a lot of people go through a lot of different kinds of crises. Some were Christians; some were not. What a difference there is! Money, position, influence, name—none of these has much bearing on a situation when the doctor begins to talk about cancer or severe lung disease or crippling, disabling heart disease. A million dollars has little meaning to an eighty-pound man who has almost lost his battle with lung cancer—but God and his faith mean everything. Such a man said recently, "Chaplain, you just don't know what the peace, the assurance of Jesus means to me today." Another stated, "It's so wonderful to know things are right between me and God and to know he is walking with me through this ordeal and will soon welcome me home." The sixty-year-old man facing open heart surgery the next day was a man of great faith. He could smile and say, "God has been good to me. I've had a wonderful life, I have nothing to lose tomorrow no matter how things turn out. If the surgery is successful I'll be rid of this pain and I'll be able to enjoy life again. If things don't work out so well, then I'll enter into a new way of life with him." This man was not putting up a front, he was not trying to impress the chaplain; he was a dedicated, committed, strong Christian, and his walk with God had begun long before his hospitalization. He knew where he had been and where he was going. The Holy Spirit was his guide.

Faith makes a difference in mental or emotional illness also. The strongest Christian can be shaken and become very emotionally upset when his life is rocked to the roots by some crisis which descends on him like a great storm. However, this person has something to hold onto. The rains come and the winds blow, but his house is built on a solid foundation—God. And his belief in God helps him to rise up and overcome this emotional illness. Sometimes a person finds God in the midst of an ordeal such as this and discovers the way out through Christ.

A young man, married, thirty-three years old, was brought to the hospital in a highly nervous condition. He was shaking, was obviously very scared, and seemed to feel threatened in the hospital setting. The chaplain visited him, and the patient told a long story of the events which had brought him to the hospital.

Several years before he and his wife had become friends with another couple. The patient had an affair with the other woman which lasted two and a half years. Then he and his family had moved some distance away and they had not heard from the other couple in over two years. One night after the evening meal he was reading the paper. There was an article on the front page about their former friends. The man had been found murdered and his wife had been arrested and charged with the crime. The patient became very upset. He felt that some way, somehow, during the investigation and trial of this other woman, she would reveal their affair. He could not eat or sleep and was unable to work. Finally he confessed to his wife. She assured him of her forgiveness, but he could not believe her. He lived with the horror of being publicly incriminated.

During several months' hospitalization he was led to seek God's forgiveness. At first he couldn't believe that God could forgive such a terrible act. He felt he could never find full forgiveness of the affair because the woman's husband was dead and he could never seek his forgiveness.

Then he discovered that God could and would forgive, and he experienced that forgiveness. His new-found faith was the greatest factor in his recovery. What a joy it was to talk with this young man and his wife and children on the day he was discharged! He was happy and confident and looking forward to a completely new way of life. His wife and children felt that husband and father had been restored to them through the grace of God. They stood in my office, and we joined in a prayer of thanksgiving for his recovery. Today, several years later, this man has had no recurrence of his emotional problems and has not been hospitalized again.

God moved in the life of this man in the midst of a great storm. He was at the breaking point but God led him back. Faith made the difference.

As a pastor and hospital chaplain I have lived in the midst of physical and mental illness for a number of years. I deal with death and dying every day. And what a great difference there is between the life of a person who is a Christian and one who is not, when the path leads uphill and life begins to cave in. The person who is not a Christian has nothing concrete to hold on to when the going gets rough. He will often muster up pseudo-courage and a false front for his own benefit and for the sake of his family. But the truth, the fright, the lostness shine through. Anxiety builds up and adds to the physical illness. And this same person, in many cases I have witnessed, dies in this spiritual condition because he wasn't man enough to admit his need of God. He rationalizes his life away, while asking why this happened to him. "Why did God allow this to happen to me?" is the classic question of the unbeliever.

On the other side of the coin is the Christian, the person who has dedicated his life to God and the way of Christ. His faith is strong and is made stronger in the midst of physical illness and impending death. He has something to hold on to; he has hope. Though saddened at the thought of separation from his family, his very soul is made to rejoice as he realizes death will be the door through which he will pass to be with Christ.

To be with a Christian, one who has complete faith and trust in God, when he or she is facing death can be one of the most beautiful, moving experiences you will ever have.

Sam was eighty-two years old and a strong, confident Christian. He had had surgery for cancer several times over a three-year period. Finally he returned to the hospital for what was to be the last time. When I visited him, he said, "Chaplain, I know I'm here to die this time. I've talked to the doctor, and we have been frank with each other. I don't feel like eating, so I do not want any food. I would like enough water to keep my mouth and throat moist. I do not want any bottles or tubes to prolong life and misery. The doctor has kindly agreed to grant these requests. I am at peace with God—I'm ready to die—I have no fear of death. Please come by as often as you can."

These last days extended into two weeks. Sam grew weaker day by day. His greetings and conversation faded, but his faith never wavered. He knew where he had been and he knew where he was going and he knew the way.

Sam's faith was the greatest factor of his life. He lived with it and by it. He called on this same faith when he came to the end of the way. His faith made all the difference in the world to him as he faced terminal illness. He said, "I believe the same

Lord whom I've served most of my life will walk with me down this lonely journey. And because of this assurance I'm not afraid."

A person's faith is the difference in life, whether it's rough or easy, whether he's well or sick, and when he comes to the end of the way. A strong faith will carry you through the storms of life.

16

The Uniqueness of the Gospel in Healing

BY THE REV. G. EDWARD BRYAN, PH.D.

Introduction

The relationship between mental illness and morality can no longer be dismissed. Traditionally, religion and medicine were fused, and healing and salvation were one in both concept and process.

Man's identity to survive as a whole being in an age of technology and depersonalization has decreased in direct proportion to his awareness of this intimate relationship of religion and medicine. Man's survival depends largely upon the understanding and internalization of his value system. No longer can we afford a dichotomy between religion and values. Rather, it is this dichotomy that has contributed to a large extent to our present "crisis" in mental health, as it is itself fragmented in its attempts to reconcile, heal, or integrate an already alienated and fragmented society.

Technology has become God[1]—we worship the computer and are facing a lost identity as we are absorbed by it. The rape and murder of our planet for economic gain is only one more form of spiritual alienation and "eco-catastrophe."[2] In this alienation man is separated not only from God but from his neighbors and also from himself.

The gospel is *unique* in therapy in supplying the unity, wholeness, healing, or salvation to this self-destructive and counterproductive, as well as self-defeating, alienation.

In spite of the microvision of this strange dilemma there is *hope*. This hope is found in the spiritual reality which, when acknowledged, inspires still more hope. This healing takes place through faith; it is through faith that mankind finds "the highest halls of human happiness." Do we lose faith? Could it be that alienation from ourselves, from our brother, from our God, is a symptom of our spiritual pathology? It is against the background of family explosions, population explosions, and sexplosions that we ask, "Is analysis the only cure?" It is against this background of disturbed Americans[3] and changing morals and changing family patterns,[4] against this background where 9,000,000 Americans are suffering from alcoholism, that we ask, "Is there any hope?"

Could it be that the heart of the human problem is still the human heart? Could it be that a return to faith in God, and consequently a faith in self under God, could be the answer? We think so. These unprecedented problems in man's history and the speed of change inviting them, are indeed complex. This phenomenon related to mental health is an area of the greatest "non-response and mal-response" and only staggers the imagination. We might well ask the question, Are there any answers? We think so.

Traditionally religion played a major part in wholeness; the holistic concept of the Jewish faith is a witness to this throughout the Old Testament. However, the secularization of religion becomes an impediment to healing when role function and identity are lost in the process.[5]

As medicine faces the rediscovery of man, one sees the mutual interdependency of religion and medicine. They stand together; alienation of the two compounds the problem and furthers the split. It is man thus dichotomized who finds neither healing nor salvation.[6]

Healing and salvation are found to be one and the same process. Carroll Wise comments upon this "wholeness" when he states, "To the extent that the organism functions as a whole, it may be said to be in a state of health. Illness arises when for whatever reason integration breaks down and the part gains control over the whole."[7] The holy scriptures are filled with experiences that link healing and salvation. Following are a few examples: God is portrayed as the Healer where he states, "For I am the Lord, your healer (Exod. 15:26)"; also where he healed Miriam of leprosy (Numbers 12:13-15). David proclaimed God as healer when he proclaimed God as the One "who heals all your diseases (Ps. 103:5)."

When Israel rebelled against God, they were told, "There is none to uphold your cause, no medicine for your wound, no healing for you (Jer. 30:13)." There are many more scriptures that refer to God as the Author of healing and not of sin or suffering. Briefly, "O Lord my God, I cried to thee for help, and thou has healed me (Ps. 30:2)." And, "As for me, I said, O Lord, be gracious to me; heal me, for I have sinned against thee! (Ps. 41:4)" and, "Bless the Lord, O my soul, and forget not all his benefits, who forgives all your iniquity, who heals all your diseases (Ps. 103:2-3)"; moreover, "He heals the brokenhearted, and binds up their wounds (Ps. 147:3)." Whatever the cause of illness and evil or sin and suffering and heartache and sorrow or sickness, the cure was in God alone as Divine Healer (Jeremiah 16:18; 17:14). It is the Western world then that has split man in two. It was Jesus Christ who said, "I came that they may have life, and have it abundantly (John 10:10)." As we look at the ministry of Jesus, we shall see how he treated man as a whole person, rather than any segment of any one part or fragmented. In the words of Robert B. Reeves, Jr.:

> Get rid of dualism; give up once and for all the notions of body and soul; attend to the behavior of the live human being in his totality; learn again to cherish him as a creature; and we may begin to save man from the damnation of a false spirituality, and recover that ancient health which is salvation. [See page 104.]

Healing, as well as preaching, characterized the ministry of the early church.[8] The healing work of Christ is intimately associated with the act of redemption.[9] Christ often referred to the relationship between healing and salvation as he spoke of sins being forgiven,[10] whether he was speaking to the paralytic or the blind.[11] Moreover, healing became an act "on behalf of God according to his will of salvation for man."[12] Man is in need, above all else, of forgiveness and reconciliation, for if his sins are not forgiven, the kingdom of God not only remains closed to him[13] but he remains alienated from his God and from himself. Weatherhead describes this process:

> It seems to me that all healing methods known to modern science, including psychological methods, are on one plane. But Christ functioned on a higher plane and used methods in a different

category. . . . His *unique* relationship to God made Him at home in the spiritual world, and when He broke into a situation of human pain and distress, of body and mind, He brought with Him the energies of the plane on which He Himself lived.[14]

This should lead one to believe that while God uses medical science, he certainly is not indebted to it. An atmosphere of trust and confidence was necessary for Christ, himself, to heal his patients It was unbelief that inhibited ἀπιστία.[15] Christ's miracles were symbolic demonstrations of God's ultimate forgiveness and reconciliation of man. It is for this reason that his healing was a "scandal on a weekday let alone on the Sabbath."[16] While it is true that Christ laid his hands on some to heal them, it was a subject of "faith."[17] It is for this reason we note early recognition by the *British Medical Journal* that "no tissue of the human body is wholly removed from the influence of spirit."[18] Furthermore, as high as 80 percent[19] of the diseases of which man suffers are referred to as psychosomatic.[20] Martin verifies this when he states:

> Whoever therefore accepts his own salvation by faith in Jesus Christ must realize that the promise applies as much to his physical as to his spiritual health. . . . The healing ministry of Jesus Christ and his work of salvation are inseparable.[21]

The cure of a certain body ailment cannot be equated with health for it may be a part of health; nor should the miracle of healing be used as an end in itself. When Christ was healing someone with his ministry, he was concerned with the total need of the person he was healing. It is God who gives the power to heal (Luke 5:17). Whatever methods he used through faith, the healing of laying on of hands or sometimes his miracles were performed at a distance. While Christ recognized medical ministry, he could not substitute it for spiritual healing. In Luke 5:31, he stated, "Those who are well have no need of a physician, but those who are sick." Furthermore, the use of medicine need not minimize the importance of faith and certainly not the power of God in the healing process.

Not only did Christ heal the sick but he commanded his disciples to do so.[22] Later on, we expected the Christian healing would continue throughout the church and the temperature of the spiritual life of the church was the index of her power to heal.[23] Origen, who died in A.D. 254, declared that spiritual healing was found in the first and second centuries but was on the decline.[24] Again, reconciliation is the end, not healing; thus the curative factor "is the forgiveness of sins."[25]

Healing in the Early Church

The practice of healing continued. "The healing of the body played an enormous part in Christian practice. It is not generally recognized that, in the pagan world at this time, getting treated for an illness was by no means easy."[26] It was at this time that the priest-physician was still operative. Some bishops were trained physicians, according to Adolf Harnack, and G. G. Dawson records this prayer for bishops: "Grant him, O Lord, to loose all bonds of the iniquity of demons, the power to heal all diseases and quickly to beat down Satan under his feet."[27]

Later, as material means came from the Greek culture and since materialistic medicine made little demand upon the faith of the believer,

> Men did not behold God working through the new methods. God was left out. The drugs acted whether or not the patient believed in God. The insidious disease of materialistic humanism set in. Man has discovered drugs! He can do without God. "Glory to man in the highest; for man is the master of things."[28]

With the advance of science, a serious conflict between science and religion began to take place.[29] The saving faith of "thy faith hath made thee whole (Matt. 9:22)" began to wane when politics and religion mixed. The pressure of secular society was too much for the church.[30] At this time the conflict began between the church and medicine and a whole history of events that are outlined in the church's annals of almost abandonment, form a position, and the medical rationale for her hostility.[31] It was also, at this time, that both the concept of God and the concept of man were distorted. Men blamed God for their sufferings.[32] A split was inevitable; Jung describes it: "The irresistible tendency to account for everything on physical grounds corresponds to the horizontal development in the last four centuries and this horizontal perspective is a reaction against the exclusively vertical perspective of the Gothic Age."[33]

It was here that medicine began to become more concerned with the disease of the person than the person of the disease.[34] It is here the danger lies in modern medicine, for it is possible in a technological society for a man to master the technique of any profession (religion or medicine) and thereby reduce himself to a mere technician. This is precisely what happens to the physician who does not recognize the soul or spiritual quality of the patient.[35] It might be stated at this point that science became to medicine what fertilizer was to farming! There was no need for God. Fortunately we shall see, following the renaissance of the onset of the Reformation, that it was not always to remain so; for the cooperation between ministers and doctors for the redemption of the whole man was yet to be seen at a future date. Early indications came from Plato, when he said:

> Medicine is not merely a science but an art. It does not consist of compounding pills, plasters, and drugs of all kinds, but it deals with the *processes* of life which must be understood before it can be guarded. . . . Character of the physician may act more powerfully upon the patient than all drugs employed.[36]

Also, it was Ambrose Perez (A.D. 1510-1590), who stated, "I treat, God heals."[37] It was in this context that Ellen G. White stated, "The mind controls the whole man. All our actions, good or bad, have their source in the mind. It is the mind that worships God and allies us to heavenly beings."[38]

The Uniqueness of the Gospel in Dealing with All Phases of Human Existence

The gospel then is not just about healing but is, rather, healing itself. Martin states:

> Thus for the church in the New Testament, healing the sick is not a means of propaganda in order to preach the Gospel of spiritual liberation; it is an intricate part of this message. . . . It is not a question of healing for the sake of healing. Healing is not an aim in itself. It has no other aim but the glorification of God.[39]

When we think of it, all whom Christ healed eventually died anyway! While Christianity contained many contrasting ideas about evil and sin and suffering, and the idea of blaming God for its origin, it also brought into this context a unique element.[40] Because of broken relationships,[41] we have broken hearts, broken bodies, broken minds, broken spirits, and broken homes—broken anything![42] In order to understand this, one must redefine sin in its relationship to God and man. Frank Kimper states, "I perceive sin to be any form of human self-expression which *fails to affirm* the infinite worth of one's neighbor as oneself."[43] Jesus said, "Love the Lord thy God with all thy heart, and with all thy soul, and with all thy mind, . . . [and] thy neighbour as thyself (Mark 12:30)."

We ask, Which comes first, one's self or one's neighbor? Or, as someone has expressed it, Love thy neighbor, he is thyself! The gospel then is not the "good news" about forgiveness, but rather forgiveness itself! This is in reality the "good news." In terms of disturbed emotions, then, we might add that "openness is to healing what secrecy is to illness." To Christ, man was a whole person in need of salvation. It is not a question of just "saving souls" but of saving men.[44] His was the concern with all that makes up the personality of man, with a whole man who was in need of redemption. Jesus said to the sick or the palsied, "Your sins are forgiven. . . . Rise, take up your bed and go home (Matt. 9:4, 6)." It is the church's task to restore medicine and theology to their original integrated relationship.[45] Christ has set the pace for settling the Greek dualism that would inhibit the fusion of religion and medicine toward its same goal of wholeness or healing. Carl Jung says, "The distinction between mind and body is an artificial dichotomy, a discrimination which is unquestionably based far more on the peculiarity of intellectual understanding than on the nature of things."[46]

Wade Boggs summarizes this concept by stating:

> There is inescapable overlapping of errors of responsibility, resulting from the obvious fact that *spiritual conditions* have an important effect upon bodily states and body states in turn affect spiritual conditions. Giving assent to this fact of body-mind interrelationship is tantamount to an admission that health is integrally related with religion.[47]

A Place for Medicine and Ministry in Healing the Emotions

The literature in both fields of psychiatry and religion is as inconclusive as it is vast.[48] The domains of psychiatry and religion are sometimes overlapping and sometimes mutually interdependent rather than mutually exclusive.[49] It is in understanding this reality that both disciplines have contributed more recently to a growing congeniality.[50] There are two causes for this growing interdependence; the first is an increasing insistence on the part of religion that "psychiatry cannot adequately pursue the whole man without taking into account the contributions religion has made available for the search."

> As a consequence, the offices of the minister are being more wisely utilized to augment the skill of the psychotherapist and the recognition of metaphysical concern as contributory neurosis and in the resolution of that concern through the resources of religion.[51]

The same type of interdisciplinary relationships exist between the psychologist and the chaplain or minister.[52] James Hillman demonstrates the potential pitfall for ministers:

> Pastoral counselors have been partly led astray in the way in which they have taken to psychology. The word "clinical" has become all but numinous; a minister's visit is a "housecall"; parishioners are "patients"; psychodynamic cure tends to replace psychological care. Yet the deep need of the individual remains. Although his need is less for mental health than for guidance of soul, he still turns to his analyst for what he might be receiving from his minister, so that analyst and minister seem each to be performing the other's task. The minister has held back from fulfilling his model of shepherd of souls, because he has felt himself to be an amateur who "hadn't enough psychology."[53]

This "identity crisis"[54] is not simply related to the general public but specifically related to confusion of identity and pastoral counsel. This replacement of "soul" by "psyche" and the professionalism following it "are beginning to do as much damage as did the ignorance and moralism about the psyche in the last century."[55] This is Hillman's way of saying the psyche cannot replace the soul. By these statements we will notice how the modern psychologist recognizes the *uniqueness* in the world of the ministry.[56] We should ask, then, if the minister himself recognizes this *unique* position?[57] Hillman states, "Where the encounter fails, all falls flat."[58] It is because of the pathology of broken communications in the relationships that healing has not transpired.

Why Medicine Needs Religion

Freud made his basic mistake in his lecture, "Philosophy of Life,"[59] where he disdains and disparages the constructs of society's philosophy that would offer a more complete tentative picture of the universe. He denies any validity of philosophy in religion and stakes out "the whole field of human activity as the exclusive province of science."[60] Modern psychiatry, in the voices of Stern and Maritain and others, rejects a limited view of Freudism.[61] While Freud proclaimed his loyalty to "the scientific Weltanschauung," he staked out the spirit and the mind as proper objects of scientific investigation but specifically rejected religion and philosophy as collaborators in proof finding. What Freud failed to notice was that, while disclaiming one religion, he promoted another—his own personal credo.[62] This unfinished world-view is not only an abstraction, but a limited one. While Freud declared that psychoanalysis does not involve itself with value judgments, others, such as Zilboorg, Masserman, and Rioch, along with Harry Stack Sullivan, support the idea that the basic questions of what man is, what it is he wants, what it is he ought to want, and what place he has in relationship to his fellowman and to society and to himself as a person, are ultimately and fundamentally religious questions. Therefore, "a psychoanalyst, more than any other professional man, must cultivate a philosophy of values."[63] Mowrer, in particular, believes that neurosis transpires because men "have repudiated their own moral strivings. This makes the undoing of repressions preeminently a moral enterprise." Pfister supports this idea by stating, "The repressed conscious state is still a more troublesome world than the known conscience . . . it is of great importance to replace the ill-advised with a clear and noble piercing voice of conscience!"[64]

At this point, the roles of the psychiatrist and the minister must not only be defined but understood in their interprofessional relationship. Modern psychiatry recognizes not only the uniqueness of the function of the minister but the ultimate necessity of a value system and further shows that life and morality cannot be separated. Moreover, morality and mental health are mutually interdependent.[65] Now we can begin to see why medicine (psychiatry) needs religion. Dr. Karl Menninger states, "The basis of all religion is a duty to love God and offer our help to His children." Psychiatry, too, is dedicated to the latter duty.[66] It is suggested that psychiatry must not only keep its bond with religion, at this point, but also with medicine, for "the healing of personality is bound so intimately with physical healing that psychotherapy should keep a tie with medicine."[67] William D. Sharpe states, "Clergymen and physicians help the family to understand the disease process, insofar as they can, and the clergyman's role may be larger because he may be closer at hand than an overworked physician at a distant hospital."[68] A recent survey showed that a majority (58 percent) of those who have emotional problems see a minister first.[69] (More recent surveys indicate 48 percent.) Harold Blake Walker states, "They recognized in practice the wholeness in man and saw him as a psycho-physical-spiritual being."[70] Walker shows three schools of thought concerning medicine and religion. The first,

> To insist that medicine and religion are two different things and therefore should have nothing to do with each other. The second, there are people who say that while religion and medicine are two different things, they may have some relationship provided the emphasis is on the differences and religion remains a junior partner in the healing enterprise. Thirdly, many of us are persuaded that religion and medicine can and should collaborate as *equals* in dealing with the ills of mankind.[71]

Dr. Franklin Ebaugh of the University of Colorado Medical School noted (as brought out by Walker):

> One third of the patients in the average hospital are there because of organic disruptions; another third are there because of a

combination of organic and emotional disturbances; and one third are there because of emotional problems. Dr. Karl Menninger goes further and says, "There is an emotional component in every illness."[72]

It is this whole way of life or life-style where people are troubled about moral issues and/or ought to be troubled about them that forces the analyst to realize concern must include *values* as part of the very path of therapy.[73] Another way the clergyman may help the psychiatrist is in understanding family conflicts, because, if a patient returns from the hospital to a hostile, guilt-ridden environment, regression is the rule and not the exception.[74]

Gordon Allport discusses this unwillingness to deal objectively with religion. Freud denied the validity of the religious process, and placed it under a severer criticism. Allport concedes, "Religion exerts all of the strongest human emotions. A religious view of the universe adds strength and stability to personality. Freud acknowledges, even while he is trying to refute, religion's claim to truth by arguments and psychoanalysis."[75] Allport shows the paradox of the psychologists who write with "the frankness of Freud or Kinsey on the sexual passions of mankind but blush and grow silent when the religious passions come into view."[76] He further argues that

> the psychologist has no right to retire from the field, since two-thirds of the adults in this country regard themselves as religious people and nine-tenths affirm belief in God. Seventy per cent of the 500 college students questioned by Allport felt that they needed some form of religious orientation or belief in order to achieve a mature philosophy of life. Seventy-five per cent of the women and 65 per cent of the men acknowledged praying, many every day.[77]

Many religious writings indicated a lack of real acquaintance with religion. There are two flaws. First, a defective understanding of religion, and second, a neglect to understand significant aspects of personality; "purposive striving."[78] Stability of personality is supported by religion in relationship to good experiences. With the coming of participants in the healing process, the therapist is drawn inescapably into the realm of values. It is then, according to Allport, "Whether he knows it or not, every psychologist gravitates toward an ontological position. Like a satellite he slips into the orbit of positivism, naturalism, idealism, personalism."[79] The openness of the therapist is important in both the intervention and re-integrative process of healing, for his own value system exerts its influence on the patient. Walters has shown that 48 percent of the therapists questioned believed that therapy does in fact directly transmit or develop value concepts in the patient.[80]

The New Breed

It is to a new recognition of the new breed of ministers and a new look at the necessity of including spiritual reality in terms of morality, mores, ethics, and morals that we now turn. Dr. Henry Turkel suggests that psychoanalysis has outlived its usefulness and believes that Freud would agree with him.[81] Turkel states:

> Nearly 50 per cent of our hospital beds, and all of our institutional beds, are occupied by mental patients. This proves that "mental therapy" as practiced by psychoanalysts is virtually valueless. In seventy years of treating mental patients through psychoanalysis, not a *single proven cure* has been found![82]

Perhaps it is for this reason that Freud's couch is giving way to the "Now" therapies.[83] Could it be that said influence is ailing and psychiatry as it has been known has failed and "will take its place within 20 years with Phrenology and Mesmerism?"[84] Could it be that this failure is due to a lack of recognition of spiritual values? Apolito believes that if God is really dead in the hearts of the patients, the psychoanalyst should be there to help with the burial and to assist the ex-religious person in filling the void that is left.[85] It is a weak argument that "psychoanalysts are not the only ones who avoid involvement in religious and moral values."[86] The argument from silence proves nothing. Apolito continues by stating that

> some leading analysts and sociologists have expressed their views about religion. Sigmund Freud stated that he was an atheist; he considered religion an illusion, and an obsessional

neurosis of mankind. He hoped that some day it would be replaced by science and reason. He was against priests practicing psychoanalysis, and he probably would have felt the same way about formerly religious analysts.[87]

It is no secret that some of the loneliest people in the world are married to each other. So a person can avoid and evade "playing one's role nicely and never getting to know the other members of the family—who also are playing roles."[88] The openness of this self-disclosure allows them to feel the therapeutic value of a loving relationship. Likewise, it is by our failure to live up to our own unacceptable standards we encounter our own self-deceptions. The minister must listen to the soul that has its secrets, because

> secrets wrongly kept act as poisons and the psyche wants to be purged of them through confession. But not all secret life is pathological, nor all shame and shyness due to sins. Secrets shared build trust and trust tames the flight-or-fight problem of distance. No wonder that there is no such thing as short psychotherapy where the soul is fully involved.[89]

Love

The importance, then, of religion in dealing with psychiatric cases is summed up in the religious attitudes toward mental health, illness, and psychiatry and the religious acts and ideas as helping devices with the syndromes of religious psychopathology and the new attitudes that are formed toward the new religion. This experimentation is taking place outside the traditional religious persuasions and therefore has been pronounced irrelevant.[90] Dr. Paul Pruyser, vice-president of the Society for the Scientific Study of Religions, is director of the Department of Education, the Menninger Foundation. He is also one of the co-authors, with Dr. Karl Menninger and Dr. Martin Mayman, of the book *The Vital Balance*.[91] Furthermore, it is because of the absence of the vital balance, the balance which cannot exist without correct concept of God in a correct concept of man, allowing one to be reconciled to both. Walters quoted Rosenthal to show how this is accomplished: "It may be that the therapist communicates his values to the patient in many *unintended*, *subtle ways*, even when trying to avoid doing so."[92] We should be careful in trading one kind of magic for another.[93] For while the therapist can feel himself to be objective and detached as a scientist, a more realistic view would see him involved and subjective or participant in his manners, influencing the patient or client by his "own basic philosophy of life."[94] Medicine needs religion because there is more personality maladjustment because of the inability to "love than for any other reason." Being also unable to love oneself or to love others at the "deepest realities of the universe, we are ill."[95] Walker tells of Freud's statement that, "In the last resort, we must begin to love in order that we may not fall ill and must fall ill, but in consequence of frustration, we cannot love. In short, every illness has a spiritual dimension that cannot be reached by physical therapy."[96] This is in harmony with Dr. Smiley Blanton's book *Love or Perish*. Sidney M. Jouard and Ardis Whitman demonstrate that it is fear that cheats us of love for in "wanting to make others like us, we may be making it impossible for them to love us."[97] Jouard further states "that if we wish to be loved, we must first prove that we have the courage to be loved."[98] He adds that "people wear masks a great deal of the time. Children don't know their parents; parents don't know their children. Husbands and wives are often strangers to each other."[99] It seems that these could be the declaration of the bankrupt condition of psychoanalysis as it is today practiced, for Apolito calls the psychoanalyst "the physician of the soul." He also believes that the psychoanalytic cure of the soul will bring about such a religious orientation. He is quoting Fromm, of course. Attempting to rid man of religion, there then has been a God substitute. "The Freudian father is a more terrifying figure than the God of the Bible. So it appears that religion, chased out through one door, sneaks back in through another door, although in disguise."[100] On the other hand we notice that while attempting to negate God in the name of science, analysts have not been able to divorce themselves from the central theme of values.

Verghese believes:

> Mental health is the capacity of an individual to form harmonious relationships with others and to participate in or contribute

constructively to changes in social environment. It is the result of a harmonious relationship of an individual with himself, with others around and with God.[101]

Verghese shows that a person may lose his capacity to have communion with God. It can happen that the spiritual dimension gets atrophied because of deliberate neglect and disuse. Verghese concludes:

> When the spiritual dimensions of personality are not satisfied, spiritual illness sets in. This spiritual illness can manifest as neuroses and personality disorders. It can also manifest as abnormal religious attitudes. Religious fanaticism and unbalanced religious life can be the result of unsolved religious conflicts. Thus, it is possible that some psychiatric patients suffer because of spiritual conflicts and the psychotherapy of these patients must be geared to consideration of spiritual values. This concept of spiritual illness emphasizes the common frontier between Psychiatry and Theology.[102]

The metamorphosis that has been taking place in psychiatry in terms of its own identity crisis is related to spiritual values.

Where Do We Go from Here?

Maturity and wholeness come through Christian growth. Cassert has stated, "Man must become what he is. It is by human effort in cooperation with God's grace that man's *uniquely* human potentials must be realized in his growth towards maturity and wholeness."[103] Although there has been considerable attention given recently to both "medicine and religion" and "religion and medicine," rarely do we see the second term employed in lieu of the first.[104] While much attention has been given recently to the concepts of the whole man and his total care, we may raise the question of whether or not adequate consideration of the religious dimension and its importance in medicine has yet been considered.[105] In order for the religious factor to be considered top priority it must be included at the curriculum level of medicine, and it is here that the contemporary medical student must learn more about human values and develop his own social conscience, thus providing total care for his patients.[106]

Part of the problem in communication between religion and medicine is based upon "hierarchy," whose higher structure is best known to religionists. It is also apparent in the "pecking order" of medicine. Because of the modus operandi of the "Peter Principle" at work, professionalism takes its toll upon the profession.[107] Both religion and medicine must look beyond the limited view of their professionalism if they are not to contribute further to this dichotomy. Moreover, Dr. Rollo May demonstrates how violence is related to the lack of power and shows our complicity in it when he says, "We know that a common characteristic of all mental patients is their powerlessness and with it goes a constant anxiety which is both cause and effect of the impotence."[108] If the integration of religion and medicine is to take place, so that the goal of integrating the patient can be realized it would be helpful to understand that both professions must not only be aware of but contribute to unity and wholeness.

The gospel says that man is saved by hope (faith).[109] When we speak of hope, we speak of toleration. Differences of religion must then be tolerated.[110] The true *uniqueness* of the gospel is, of course, charity. Suffice it to say, charity means love and this can be referred to only in the ἀγαπέ sense of the New Testament.

The Uniqueness of the Minister or Religious Leader

Linn not only believes that the religious leader is an indispensible member of the treatment team but that the psychiatrist, psychologist, social caseworker, and members of allied disciplines need his help, just as he needs their help for completion.[111]

Dr. A. Dixon Weatherhead believes that it is the religious who can help make the hospital a place where hospitality may be found. He thus serves an *unique* function, treating the whole individual, "his body, his mind and his spirit."[112] It is to this uniqueness that the religious worker must address himself.[113]

James Hillman speaks of the "inner-darkness of the unconscious" as a moral problem. It is in this light that the gospel is unique. When religion and psychology are in conflict there is a question of who has claim to the soul, those who uphold morality or those who analyze it away. Sir Thomas Brown, physician from Norwich, put it this way, "*I cannot go to cure the body of my patient, but I forget my profession and call upon God for his soul.*"[114]

Conclusion

The unprecedented problems of mankind in rapid change, as related to the relationship of religion and mental health, demand our attention. Because of the need for increased training for mental health specialists, the religious leader must first of all know his identity. Secondly, he will understand his unique function in therapy. It is to this uniqueness a religious worker must address himself.

> As wielding an *unique* instrument, he helps where other members of the team cannot help. Their training forbids them from trespassing on the religious domain. Similarly, the role of the religious leader on the team is such that he cannot assume the roles of the other members without diluting and impairing his own. . . . It is also clinically clear that psychiatric treatment need have no adverse effect upon the religious feelings and practices, but on the contrary, can and does enhance a person's capacity for religious faith and fellowship.[115]

We conclude, then, that the uniqueness of the gospel contributes to the integration of medicine and religion.

In our present fragmented society the place of religion in healing has been distorted and usurped, whereas a true understanding of their relationship makes the role of religion unique.

> The Gospel is *unique* in providing faith, hope and love. This *uniqueness* has been demonstrated both by religionists, clinical psychologists and psychiatrists. It is further shown through selected case histories of both alcohol and other drug problems that often the Gospel only was the cure (and, therefore, was *unique*), while other therapies totally failed in assessing the spiritual reality behind the illness or spiritual need necessary for recovery. It could be suggested then, that religionists return to their role, and likewise cooperate with other professionals, as they attempt to search for causes which may only be explained and interpreted in terms of values and meaning, which is ultimately a question for religion and, therefore, UNIQUE.[116]

17

The Relationship of the Human Spirit to the Holy Spirit in the Process of Healing

BY THE REV. JOHN E. PENNINGTON, JR.

It is the purpose of this study to postulate a hypothesis concerning the relationship of the Holy Spirit to the human spirit in the process of healing. There has been much written concerning the Holy Spirit, less written concerning the human spirit, still less written concerning their relationship, and practically nothing with regard to their relationship to the healing process. Therefore the following essay reflects a personal compilation of ideas reinforced by the thoughts of scholars on the individual subjects of human spirit, Holy Spirit, and the healing process. The hypothesis that I wish to develop is that there is a direct relationship between the Holy Spirit and the human spirit with regard to healing, and furthermore that it is the human spirit which determines to a large degree the effectiveness of the Holy Spirit in the healing of individuals.

I begin this work with the basic Christian presupposition that God continues to work through many different means to bring about the physical as well as spiritual well-being of his highest creation, man himself. This he does through the person of the Holy Spirit. Man, in turn, can help or hinder the process. "There are two sides of our relation to the Holy Spirit. We have a part to play in his activities. . . . But if we may help, we may also hinder. We may put barriers in his way and by so much may defeat his purpose."[1] As Georgia Harkness has said, "Openness, sensitivity to God and human need, earnest search for the will of God and obedience when we find it, are indispensable to the human spirit if the Holy Spirit is to find entrance."[2]

The basic problem lies in the definition of the spirit of man. It is possible to go to great lengths in discussing the analysis of contemporary thought on the nature of the human spirit. But as George Hendry put it:

> Throughout the greater part of its history, Christian theology has been chiefly concerned with the doctrine of the Holy Spirit, ... and in this it has been faithful to the emphasis of the New Testament; it has shown little interest in the question how this spirit is related in essence and operation to the spirit that is in man, and in this too it has followed the example of the New Testament.[3]

Martin Luther described the spirit as "the highest, deepest, noblest part of man, by which he is able to grasp incomprehensible, invisible, and eternal things."[4] Others, like Karl Barth, while not denying that man has spirit, have designated man as the recipient of God's spirit but in no sense the possessor of his own spirit. This denial of created spirit in man on the part of theologians, both ancient and modern, may be traced back to Augustine and his one-sided conception of God's grace. Indeed, most of the Reformers looked upon God as one who descends upon the object of man.

But for our practical purposes we will consider man's spirit, somewhat as did Luther, as being that part of man which makes up his "person." It is the part of man which enables him to form attitudes on his own and to respond to the Holy Spirit.

> The Holy Spirit does not annihilate our spirits, but bears witness with our spirits. And the Holy Spirit does not destroy the freedom of our spirits, but restores it by changing their false freedom from God into that true freedom for God, which is the glorious liberty of the children of God.[5]

Jesus was certainly aware of the spirit of man. He recognized the importance of forgiveness for guilt, the need for a faith that led to an attitude of believing one could be healed, and the power of suggestion when dealing with those who were ill.

> If we consider Jesus' total teaching about God and the importance of man's relationship to God, we shall be led to the conclusion that Jesus was concerned to restore the physical, mental, and spiritual harmony of the whole personality of the sufferer,

by placing him in a new and right relation to God, to his neighbor, and to himself.[6]

And if the purpose of Jesus' healing ministry was to reveal the compassionate love of God for mankind, then there is every reason to believe that his work continues through the Holy Spirit today. Our advancements in medical know-how bear examples just as miraculous as those in the days of Jesus. It is indeed just as miraculous to think that today through the knowledge of medical science we can prevent by use of vaccinations as well as cure by means of antibiotics many diseases which were deadly at the time of Jesus and the early church.

As a matter of fact, modern scientific methods are superior to the methods used by Jesus and the early church in that they involve the true compassion, massive generosity, and self-giving of individuals for their fellowman. John Hick has said that the necessity for man to help suffering fellowman evokes the unselfish kindness and goodwill which are among the highest values of personal life.[7]

The Holy Spirit does work through man, then, to bring about healing, and in this very important sense all healing is divine. Perhaps we would rather see the healing take place by the form of outright miracles. I have often been asked by members of a young adult Sunday school class, "Why don't we have those miraculous healings any more?" We tend to be like those addressed by Jesus in John 4:48 who couldn't really believe unless they could see great and wonderful works. The attitude is, "Give us a miracle, Lord, so we'll know you're still there."

William Barclay, in his commentary, *The Acts of the Apostles*, treats the miracles of healing in the early church by saying that there is no denying that such events did take place. According to Barclay, we see them no more because they were only needed as an initial outbreak of Christianity to get the work of the church off to a good start. Also in the days just following the death of Jesus, willingness to believe was at a much higher level. But Barclay would question those who would dogmatically say that miracles have stopped in our own day of medical technology.[8] Indeed, the miracles are in front of our faces. We have but to open our eyes.

We should look today for signs which effectively express the divine spirit of compassion in the area of healing primarily from doctors, surgeons, dentists, medical scientists, psychiatrists, nurses, and technicians who have put forth sacrificial efforts to learn the principles, the techniques, the means by which God heals, in order that they may cooperate with him.[9]

It is here that the church needs to be involved again in the business of healing today. Through faith and intercessory prayer we may continue to recognize and claim the healing powers of God made manifest most often in medical science. The powers are ours for the asking. How may the church realize her healing ministry as it was once recognized by the early church?

The Church must recognize and accept her calling by Christ to such a ministry. She must understand herself as the saving framework in which profound healing takes place. . . . Here must be expressed that acceptance and affection, that concern and compassion of Christ, that binds up the wounds of the world.[10]

The early church was very effective in the healing ministry because the early Christians recognized and accepted their calling in this regard. That day is over, although it may very well return some day. As long as the church exists there is the possibility of miracles from God. But the church will return to the kind of miracles displayed in apostolic days only if we return to the faith and expectancy of that time. Until then God continues to work miracles through the power of the Holy Spirit through medical achievements, because when people go to the doctor they do expect some results.

This idea of expectation is a part of the all-important human spirit that cooperates with the healing power of the Holy Spirit. With the proper attitude, man can enhance his healing process. Doctors have been heard to say on many occasions that it is a patient's own will to live that often proves to be a vital factor in that patient's recovery. When a person submits himself to the providential care of God by putting his trust in God, he also places trust and confidence in the doctors who care for him. This patient is the kind whose spirit cooperates with the Holy Spirit to enhance the healing process. There is a certain obedience possible in the face of suffering unlike that known at any other time to man. It is precisely at this time that one whose spirit is most cooperative realizes his or her total dependence upon God. It is this patient, most often, who makes the best possible recovery.

Now I would not be so blind as to overlook the fact that not all who experience healing even know God, much less give him the cooperation of their human spirit. All I can say to this point is that God's healing grace, like his redeeming grace and sustaining grace, is abundant, and God makes his rain to fall upon the just and unjust. Also, there are many whose spirit is most cooperative who fail to be healed of their physical affliction. I will deal with this problem a bit later. What I am saying at this point is that the proper response of the spirit of man to the problem of suffering can and does in many cases effect a speedier recovery. It is public knowledge that "physicians have always known that the emotional life (or spirit of man) has something to do with illness."[11]

On the other hand, a negative response by the spirit of man can interfere with the healing process of the Holy Spirit. Sickness may be best understood as a form of behavior of the ongoing self. Sickness is not the invasion of disease organisms, according to Robert B. Reeves, Jr., but how we respond to this invasion.[12] When a patient has little faith and becomes permanently bitter and resentful toward God and/or the doctor and those who are attempting to minister to him, this lack of spiritual cooperation on the part of the patient may well interfere with the healing process.

A number of doctors, among them Dr. Arnold A. Hutschnecker, an internist-psychiatrist who has studied the mind-matter interplay from both points of emphasis, believe that psychic factors (man's spirit) play a large part in causing death from cancer. Just as our body chemistry can react to stimulation, let's say, by a step up in the flow of adrenalin, so it can react to the wish to die by a slowdown, then a halt, in the body processes.

Dr. Hutschnecker calls this the "negative state of stress." He says that "cancer patients die when they are overcome by a state of futility and hopelessness."[13] A negative spirit toward unpleasant situations can be the root cause of many psychosomatic illnesses. Dr. Hutschnecker has said that "within the framework of our individual constitution, we ourselves choose the time of illness, the kind of illness, the course of illness, and its gravity."[14]

Of course, the only way a person may truly be healed is to be healed as Jesus healed, physically and spiritually. There is an important relationship between the physical, emotional, and spiritual dimensions of man. Only when the Holy Spirit gives strength to the human spirit is one ultimately made "whole." "Certainly the Church and medical science are moving in the right direction today in attempting to combine the best information gleaned from the disciplines of science with the health-giving resources of the Christian religion."[15]

But what of those patients whose spirit is most open and receptive to the Holy Spirit, yet in spite of their cooperation their condition only worsens? Would this contradict all that has been said thus far? Certainly not. There are some diseases for which we have no cure. Even those people healed by Jesus and the early church died eventually of something. No one, regardless of spirit, can live forever.

We *can* say that these persons receive the sustaining grace, as did Paul, which enables them to go on with living, "thorn or no thorn," and eventually bear that which they must with the help of the living Lord. Moreover, that person's human spirit can be used by the Holy Spirit to carry out a healing ministry of its own. No one involved in such a situation can come away from the experience unchanged. As J. Burnett Rae has said:

> The patient himself may become a source of healing. Every believer in the healing power and love of God, certainly everyone who has experience of this, is himself potentially a healer. When combined with medical knowledge and skill the possibilities are very great. . . . Most doctors can tell of certain sick rooms from which they never come away without feeling that they themselves have been refreshed and healed; when one man believes, another catches the flame.[16]

When a patient attains this ability we cannot say that the Holy Spirit has failed with regard to the healing process. This is the person who like Christ himself is able to endure his or her affliction and see beyond it.

My remarks may be substantiated by a number of physicians, including the editor and compiler of this book, Dr. Claude A. Frazier of Asheville, North Carolina. Dr. Frazier has written Sunday school lessons for the Baptist state paper of North Carolina and conducts a weekly newspaper feature in the *Asheville Citizen-Times* dealing with religious subjects, as well as a periodic television program. On the other hand, I am sure there are many who would place less emphasis on the human spirit in its relationship to the Holy Spirit, perhaps even less emphasis on the Holy Spirit itself in relation to healing. But of all the words that have been written by doctors with reference to this subject, none express my thesis better than those of Dr. J. Burnett Rae, Consulting Physician to England's Croydon General Hospital. With his remarks I conclude.

> There is that in us which is deeper than the experience of our senses, deeper than the intellect, the core and center of our personality. It is so much ourselves that we can never know it as we can know our mental capacities or our moral character, because it is itself the knower—the subject which can never be object—but it is the point where we are in contact with the Divine Spirit. It is there that the Spirit himself beareth witness with our spirit, that we are children of God. It is there that the healing and sustaining powers of the Divine Spirit operate, unifying and giving vitality to all our human powers; and it is from this center also that we go out to fulfill in our lives the Divine purpose.[17]

Bibliography

Barclay, William (ed.) *The Acts of the Apostles.* Philadelphia: Westminster Press, 1957.

Boggs, Wade H., Jr. *Faith Healing and the Christian Faith.* Richmond: John Knox Press, 1956.

Come, Arnold B. *Human Spirit and Holy Spirit.* Philadelphia: Westminster Press, 1952.

Edmonds, Mim Randolph. "Tell Me Who You Are and I'll Tell You Where You'll Ache," *Glamour* Magazine, April 1970, p. 62.

Hagen, Kristofer. *Faith and Health.* Philadelphia: Fortress Press, 1961.

Harkness, Georgia. *The Fellowship of the Holy Spirit.* Nashville: Abingdon Press, 1966.

Hendry, George S. *The Holy Spirit in Christian Theology.* Philadelphia: Westminster Press, 1965.

Hick, John. *Evil and the God of Love*. New York: Harper & Row, 1966.
Jones, D. Caradog. *Spiritual Healing*. London: Longmans, Green and Co., 1955.
Lewis, Edwin. *The Ministry of the Holy Spirit*. Nashville: Tidings Press, 1954.
Miller, Paul M. *How God Heals*. Scottdale, Pa.: Herald Press, 1960.
Reeves, Robert B., Jr. Paper presented as a lecture at North Carolina Memorial Hospital in Chapel Hill, North Carolina.
Scott, Ernest F. *I Believe in the Holy Spirit*. Nashville: Abingdon Press, 1958.
Starkey, Lycurgus M., Jr. *The Holy Spirit at Work in the Church*. Nashville: Abingdon Press, 1965.
Young, Richard K., and Albert L. Meiburg. *Spiritual Therapy*. New York: Harper & Brothers, 1960.

18

The Experience of Healing Prayer

BY CANON H. L. PUXLEY

My wife and I knew nothing of prayer healing until we went to India as a very young newly married couple in 1932. We had both grown up in Christian homes, she in Canada and I in England. She had never had any particular problems of faith; I had discarded the whole thing during my final year at Eton but had found my way back to a thoroughly intellectualist position through studying the philosophy of Immanuel Kant three years later at Oxford. In 1932 I had just completed my first book, *A Critique of the Gold Standard,* the fruit of a three-year research fellowship in the Yale Graduate School; married a girl from Toronto; and set sail for India with her to teach economics at a Christian college in Agra.

Within a fortnight of landing, I went down with amoebic dysentery. Sulfa drugs and antibiotics were still unknown, and there was little to mitigate the misery and danger of the disease. An uncle of mine had some years earlier died of dysentery while serving in the army in India, and I had just been visiting another young Englishman, a physicist on the college staff, who had been in the local hospital for weeks with the disease, waiting hopefully to regain enough strength to be repatriated to England. Small wonder if my wife and I were scared enough to try anything!

Thus when the wife of the principal with whom we were staying came to our room, the night before I was to go to hospital, and said, "You'd better pray about this. You're going to find it hard to remain fit in India without the support of the power of prayer," we fell to with a will. Within a few moments I had my first experience of "being healed." The fullness of this experience always defies description, but briefly I would say that, through a palpable exchange of pain and discomfort for physical well-being and through quite a sudden total relaxation and reassurance after the hours of tension and fear, I *knew* that I was well again.

Next day I went to hospital as arranged, though all bleeding had stopped. I was subjected to a number of tests. In mid-afternoon a doctor came to my room and said almost angrily, "Are you the man who is supposed to have dysentery? We can't find anything wrong with you!" I was kept in hospital for a few days, under observation and rebuilding my strength, but I had no recurrence of the disease and was finally discharged as perfectly fit.

This was the beginning of a series of experiences which continue to this day. After this first vivid lesson, my wife and I learned to *expect* to be kept well by prayer, or to be healed when illness struck, as it frequently did during our fourteen years in India. Of course, we always sought medical assistance when indicated, believing that God means us to help ourselves and to avail ourselves of all that he has revealed to mankind about the laws governing his universe. But often isolation or the suddenness with which illness can strike in Asia would compel us to rely primarily on prayer, and time and again our reliance was justified.

Then came a day when "it didn't work." It was our fourth monsoon in Agra, a season when for over two months temperature and humidity hover between 80 and 90 day and night. My fair skin, wet continuously day and night, would always develop prickly heat, and in 1936 this led to a series of boils, culminating in a carbuncle in my back. I found myself back in hospital again for an uncomfortable operation. But worse than any pain from the surgeon's knife was the anguish of "failing" in prayer. What had I done? Had I fallen into some grievous sin? Would God never hear me again?

One never knows the total answer to this kind of problem this side of eternity; if we knew all the answers, we should already have attained godhead. But during this particular experience I gradually reached two convictions, which have continued to satisfy me through all the many occasions since when I have had to accept the answer "No" to my petitions or intercessions.

First, it is possible to become brash and cocksure in one's confidence that one will always be kept healthy. We continue to be creatures of space and time while in this flesh. When I persuade myself that through prayer I have become "superman" and can work a sixteen-hour day every day through an Agra monsoon, even in God's service, I am "tempting the Lord my God." It is always he who heals, not my faith or devotion, still less some automatic slot machine with a push button labeled "Prayer." His healing comes as part of a total living relationship of day-to-day, ideally moment-to-moment, dependence of loving creature on loving Creator, loving child on loving Father, and that relationship can be damaged by a too-ready assurance that healing will always come when requested. Indeed, it is quite difficult to maintain a proper balance between the joyous assurance which comes from the experience of healing and the ready dependence which has to characterize our relationship with our Father if we are to "receive the kingdom of God as little children [receive]."

Secondly, mankind as a whole learns more through pain than through health. It is significant that the two most climactic moments in our temporal history, birth and death, are generally associated with pain. It is, of course, only through pain that we learn to observe physical laws. Leprosy is a constant demonstration of how inexorably man maims himself once he has lost the capacity to suffer pain. "The burnt child dreads the fire." But apart from these basic physical illustrations from daily living, many of us, some more than others, need the experience of pain, psychic or spiritual as well as physical, if we are to grow. A missionary on the staff of the Botany Department in our college at Agra used to use a telling allegory. When the Jumna River which flows through Agra ran low at the beginning of the hot weather before the melting snows of the Himalayas refreshed it, market gardeners used to use its bed to grow a gourd called "lauki." My friend discovered from measurements that this lauki would hardly grow at all during the hours of sunlight, but that its girth had always increased considerably between dark and dawn. Basking idly in the sunshine, it was storing up resources with which to grow in the hours of darkness. So it is, he would say, with the Christian soul; and I would have to testify that the most outstanding learning experiences of my life have all been associated with pain, mental or physical. With no affectation I would say that I thank God as heartily for my periods of suffering as for the much longer periods of glorious, joyous sunshine.

God had another very important lesson to teach us during

those early years of learning to look to him directly for health. If he had handed us the weapon of prayer with which to fend off disease from our own lives, he had also handed it to us to be used on behalf of others. The first time this was borne in upon us was during an early summer holiday in Kashmir. We were camping at a place called Sonemarg, near the head of a magnificent Himalayan valley, and were on our way back to our tents from a mountain scramble one afternoon when we emerged on a grassy ledge where some Gujars (gypsy herdsmen) were camping. A group of them were standing outside one of their lean-tos engaged in earnest conversation when they spotted us. They promptly approached us, told us that one of their company was lying in the lean-to, seriously ill, and urged us to give him some "Western medicine." My instinctive reply was that I was not a doctor and that I had no medicine, but with their pathetic confidence in the wisdom of any European they continued to urge us to go and see the man. Finally, one of them said, "If you'll just go and look at him, he'll feel better."

At this we suddenly realized how close we were to the situation in which our Lord was constantly finding himself during his earthly ministry, and we had to respond. We went with trepidation into the dark and evil-smelling lean-to and there saw a man who seemed to us at death's door, probably, my wife guessed, from pneumonia. I spoke gravely to them and asked that one of them should accompany us back to our camp, where we would give him some medicine. We had some Horlick's malted milk powder, which we felt could not possibly do the man any harm. We poured a little into a clean envelope and gave it to the man who had come with us with solemn instructions to mix "as much as will cover a half rupee" with warm water and give it to his brother at sundown and again next morning and evening. Then we sent him away and fell to prayer. Three days later we were sitting outside our tents when a group of Gujars came by. Two of them recognized us and, breaking away from their companions, came running up the hill to greet us. "How is your brother?" I asked with some apprehension. "Oh, he's fine," one replied. "He's up and about again now, so we've left him and his family and are going back to our own pasture."

This incident also proved to be the beginning of a series which continues to this day. While I would emphasize strongly that here we have learned to receive the answer "No" more frequently than when dealing with our own health, there is a joyous list where we have received a ringing affirmative. A woman in a Canadian parish was in the throes of her third miscarriage when I happened in purely by accident; she and her husband and I prayed with maximum earnestness, and the baby that was so nearly lost that day is now a healthy young woman.

A few years ago when I was preaching a mission in a town in Nova Scotia and had, as is my wont, touched on the healing ministry one evening, a middle-aged couple approached me and told me that their daughter in her early twenties had just been found to have a hole in her heart and had to face a serious operation. They also believed in the power of prayer and undertook to partner my wife and me in daily intercession until the time for the operation. An incidental fact of possible significance in this case was that the girl was just the age of our own daughter, and this somehow made it easier to pray with power. On the evening of the day that she was admitted to hospital, I received an almost hysterical phone call from the father. A last-minute examination had revealed that the girl's condition had changed and that an operation would not now be necessary.

One of our own sons was in the third year of a Rhodes Scholarship at Oxford when he wrote to us to say that he had not been feeling well since returning from an Easter vacation in Ireland. Suddenly one afternoon in May I received a transatlantic phone call from the principal of his college to say that he was seriously ill in hospital and that I should consider flying over. My wife flew the following day and went straight to the hospital in Oxford to be greeted by a doctor with the news that our son had a galloping type of Hodgkin's disease and that there was no hope. She rang me up and said, "He's just wasting away before our eyes, and there appears to be nothing that anybody can do about it." But of course there was—prayer. A great volume of prayer went up for him from our many friends who believe in this ministry. For ten days the only change in my wife's news came when one doctor suggested the faint possibility, discounted by the others, that the trouble might be tubercular. Then suddenly I received a cable: "Diagnosis changed to tuberculosis of peritoneum." From that moment, with changed treatment, my son returned to complete health, which he has enjoyed ever since.

Faulty medical diagnosis? How could a group of some of England's best doctors have greeted a distraught mother who had just flown the Atlantic with a verdict of Hodgkin's disease and stuck to that diagnosis for ten more days unless they had been sure?

So far, all the instances of intercessory healing that I have cited have concerned people who knew they were being prayed for, and who could cooperate to some degree or other. With our growing knowledge of psychosomasis, it is obviously open to anyone to claim that there is nothing miraculous or supernatural about such cases, but that the restoration of confidence to the mind of a patient who has faith would be sufficient to restore health to his body. This really becomes a question for the medical profession, and I certainly would not claim sufficient medical knowledge to say yea or nay, though I hope to give reasons later for finding it easier to believe in the intervention of a cause outside normal physical laws. However, when healing occurs in a person who is unaware that prayer is being offered, or who perhaps has no faith at all through which to cooperate, we are surely dealing with a category of cases for which there is no known explanation possible. It is for this reason that I personally always prefer to speak of "prayer healing" rather than "faith healing"; faith healing may result, and undoubtedly frequently has resulted, purely from the powerful influence of a patient's mind over his body; prayer healing covers also those cases where no such explanation is possible.

My wife and I have been vouchsafed certain experiences in this category also. The most vivid that I recall, because the earliest, occurred again during our India days. We had gone to spend a short holiday with another young English couple in a somewhat remote country town, where the husband was a district magistrate, representative of the British administration. The evening we arrived, we found our host preoccupied over a young Swedish boy whose widowed mother was the local missionary. The boy had been out with his mother touring the district on mission business when he had been taken ill. By the time his mother brought him back to town pneumonia had set in, and, in those pre-sulfa days, the boy was sick unto death. At the request of the doctor at the little town hospital, our host had sent to the nearest city for an oxygen cylinder, but it would take at least two days to arrive, and it was doubtful whether the boy would live that long. My wife and I, who were looking forward to our own first child, felt strangely moved by this story, and, though we knew nothing of this family, of whom we had never even heard before, we felt impelled to pray earnestly for that boy that night. It was my first experience of a feeling with which I have become familiar since, a sense of reassurance that our prayer was receiving a positive response. Next morning by breakfast time our host, to whom we had said nothing of our prayer vigil, had already been over to the hospital and was bursting to tell us that the boy had made a remarkable recovery during the night and was now out of danger; he had even canceled the oxygen cylinder. Unwittingly he said, "The doctor says it's a miracle!"

Once again it has to be readily admitted that in this category also a negative answer is frequently received. It perhaps stands to reason that healing should be aided by the conscious processes of the patient's mind. Petitionary prayer, where a patient with a firm faith is praying for his own recovery, is naturally the "easiest" form of healing prayer, followed by intercessory prayer for a faithful patient who knows that he is being prayed for and is prepared to cooperate. But when prayer of the third category, where the patient is unconscious or otherwise unaware that prayer is being offered, is answered in the affirmative time and again, it becomes impossible not to believe in divine intervention.

What are we to say to all these things? The foregoing instances have been cited factually from the experience of one married couple over a space of forty years. They are simply examples of a large number of other cases that could have been mentioned. Skeptics, even if they do not question the veracity or accuracy of the stories related, will still dismiss any supernatural interpretation by attributing healing either to psychosomasis or to coincidence: "the patient would have got well anyway."

I am only too ready to admit the power of psychosomasis—and to rejoice in it. Undoubtedly, one's mental outlook can, and regularly does, have a marked effect on one's physical health. I have no doubt that the remarkably good health that my wife and I have generally enjoyed has been due in no small measure to the optimistic outlook that our reliance on God for health has given us. I am therefore equally prepared to see this law in operation in other people's bodies and am sure that it is always present to some degree wherever *faith* healing occurs. I would only offer two observations.

First, religious faith is very helpful, and in many cases indispensable, in generating the positive feeling of confidence and reassurance in a patient's mind. When I was still a schoolboy, a Frenchman called Coué made a great reputation as a healer. His prescription was that each morning upon rising a person should say vigorously, "Every day, and in every way, I am becoming better and better." Many people claimed to find this helpful as a way of *keeping* healthy; it was not so convincing to a person who had fallen sick! As against any such secular device, how much more effective to urge one who believes in the God and Father of our Lord Jesus Christ that he should *expect* him to listen to prayer and to restore his body to health if it be his will! Here religion and psychosomasis play a partnership.

But secondly, it strains the credulity of anyone who has seen literally countless instances of healing following prayer to be told that these instances are always attributable either to unaided psychosomasis or to chance. This is particularly true when a much more plausible explanation is to hand. It is to that explanation that we now turn for the remainder of this chapter.

I have already spoken of healing as being part of a total pattern of life with God in the joyous dependence of loving creature on loving Creator, loving child on loving Father. *If* the general picture which Jesus gives is of the God who created and sustains this universe as being "more like the heart of a loving Father than like anything else we know" (and it is, of course, beyond the scope of this chapter to argue that this is so), then what could be more consonant with that picture than that this God should at all times be deeply concerned with the welfare of his human creation, as he once showed himself to be in the incarnation and crucifixion. If this picture is misleading, of course the entire Christian faith falls to the ground. If, on the other hand, it is true, and if the conviction of Christians that the basic Reality is a Father-God who created mankind in his own image to be children of his love, and who was prepared to send his own Son to the gallows for their sake, is valid, then why do we need to search any further than answered prayer as the explanation of events such as those that I have recounted above? To a professing Christian the explanation that they were all pure coincidences, except insofar as the patients' own minds effected cures in their bodies, is by contrast so fantastic as to appear simply laughable.

It is surprising that the whole subject of prayer has in recent years become a matter of such difficulty to so many professing Christians. This is no doubt due to a combination of the recent spread of skepticism throughout the Western world and of an inadequate apprehension of the fundamentals of the faith, which has too often been identified with a mere code of ethics.

A consistent résumé of the whole picture might be briefly stated as follows: God the Creator, being himself Person, could not be satisfied with a purely mechanical universe, however magnificent and majestic beyond man's limited comprehension. He therefore set in train the events which led with the passage of the aeons to the evolution of Homo sapiens, man made in the image of God, bearing a tiny imprint of the Imago Dei, the image of God himself. This image is human personality, conditioned by heredity and environment, but ultimately like God himself, autonomous. God took a vast risk in thus granting man autonomy; he had to do it if he desired a person to love rather than a thing, but in creating man to live with him as a member of his loving family he also gave him power to go to hell if he chose.

One of God's most earnest desires in evolving man was that the creature would freely choose to talk to him, in just the same way as a good earthly father longs for open rapport with his children. For this purpose he gave him prayer, the direct channel of communication between him and man. Just as a wise earthly father would neither wish nor attempt to dictate every word that his child must say to him, but waits, sometimes anxiously, for the child to choose for himself to say the right thing, and rejoices when he does, so also with God. He does not force us to ask him for that which he sees all too well that we need; to do so would be to outrage the very personality that he had so laboriously created and to violate our God-given autonomy. But when we turn to him out of our own love for him and gratitude for all that he has given us and seek to give him our thanks and adoration *and* to tell him our needs, how can we but expect him to listen? "If ye then, being evil, know how to give good gifts unto your children, how much more shall your Father which is in heaven give good things to them that ask him (Matt. 7:11)?"

Man alone of all creation is not totally at home in this world of space and time. In spite of his awareness of his conditioning by the forces of heredity and environment, he knows himself to be ultimately free, free to make his own decisions and free to be creative—or destructive. In order to encourage man's autonomy and creativeness, God modifies for man the laws which govern the rest of creation. The sun *must* rise and set each day; the waters *must* flow down to the sea; but man is free to make his own decisions and to regulate his own conduct, even if within limitations. God is a God of order and will not interfere capriciously with the laws that he himself has made to govern the natural universe; he will not of his own accord interfere with the law of gravity which is sending a rock hurtling toward my head. But one of his basic laws in dealing with man is that when man, made in his own image, turns to him with a prayer of petition or intercession which is in line with his will, this, as it were, opens a trapdoor into this spatiotemporal universe through which the finger of God may come, no longer capriciously now, to bring about something which would not have occurred in the ordinary process of nature without that prayer. Unless my petition were capable of bringing about something which would not have occurred but for my praying, what is the point of my asking God for anything at all? Either my prayer can be an instrument for the miraculous or it becomes a senseless, or even deceptive, exercise in spiritual muscle-flexing.

This rationale of prayer in general furnishes the one entirely satisfactory explanation of the power of healing prayer. The fact that God will not always answer all our prayers affirmatively makes not the least difference to the argument. God who sees the entire picture knows far better than we what is really good for us or for those for whom we pray; he must often hear us asking for things which would not contribute to our welfare at all. But the conviction that he wants us to talk to him, to praise him, to thank him, to listen to him, *and* to tell him our wants as they appear to us, and that he will always answer "yes" or "no" to everything that we ask him, is a far more persuasive explanation of the observed facts to a believing Christian than any amount of coincidence or psychosomasis. In fact, if such a conviction were *not* possible for us, our whole view of the universe and of our daily lives would fall far short of what an adequate apprehension of the Christian revelation entitles us to expect.

Ultimately, it is as a constituent of this whole life lived daily in joyous obedience to, and communion with, a loving heavenly Father rather than simply in the fact of healing itself that healing prayer comes into its true focus. Physical suffering is not the ultimate evil in life, and, per contra, physical healing is not man's deepest need. But as we gradually grow in the practice of the daily walk with God in the total conscious assurance that "this is my Father's world," that he has made it for us to live in as his children, that he loves us beyond anything that we can imagine, and that he sent his Son to die on the cross as evidence of this love, it becomes the most natural thing in the world that we should expect him to give us health, that we should ask him to do so and to free us from disease if and when it strikes, and that the joyous assurance of the rightness of this expectation becomes one more part of the total evidence.

Of course man remains mortal. A day must come in the life of each one of us when no amount of praying will exempt us from death. But even then we shall have the assurance, based on rational grounds as much as on any "leap of faith," that we are in the hands of One who sees the whole story and who, in the light of the cross, will go to any lengths for our welfare. We shall know that any suffering entailed is teaching us the last lessons needed to tailor us for eternity, and that our Father will himself, if we ask him, determine the "best" day for our departing.

> And so beside the silent sea
> I wait the muffled oar;
> No harm from Him can come to me
> On ocean or on shore.[1]

19
The Church's Ministry of Healing

BY THE REV. EDWARD WINCKLEY, O.S.L.

Thirty years ago, nonmedical religious healing, the kind of healing demonstrated by our Lord Jesus Christ on the shores of Galilee, in Capernaum, and in Jerusalem, was widely called "faith healing," but the expression tended to put too much responsibility on the sufferer. Over the years since then, in cycles of about five years each, the name has been changed to "spiritual healing," "divine healing," "Christian healing," and, now, "the church's ministry of healing." Perhaps the best name for this work is "Christian healing," because it is the method by which Christ healed, and it is surely the way he intended his followers to obey his command: "Heal the sick (Matt. 10:8)."

The main means of healing practiced by the church today are the ministry of the Word proclaiming the healing gospel, followed by the laying on of hands; anointing with oil (Holy Unction); intercession (the prayer of faith); and the Sacrament of Holy Communion, ministered for the body as well as the soul. In some churches, confession and absolution are often used in the healing ministry.

Jesus healed "all manner of sickness and all manner of disease (Matt. 4:23)." He gave sight to the blind, hearing to the deaf, speech to the dumb. He told a man with a withered arm to stretch it out, and it was immediately restored. He told a paralyzed man to walk, and at once he was able to do so. He told a woman with a crooked back (slipped disc?) to stand upright, and she responded. He cured a woman with an internal disorder. He healed skin disease (leprosy). After meeting him, the insane became rational. It seems that there flowed out from Jesus a power that recreated the sick, as if he were the source of life. All the narratives recording his healing miracles state that faith was exercised either by the sufferer or by someone who came to Jesus on the sick person's behalf. Next to the person of Jesus himself, faith is still the most important factor in Christian healing today.

The first apostles took Jesus at his word. The Acts of the Apostles relates many healing miracles as wonderful as those recorded in the Gospels. There is a very good reason for this—these later miracles were also wrought by our Lord, although in his post-Pentecostal, invisible form and through human agents. After death by crucifixion, Jesus was alive after resurrection and returned at Pentecost to live in and amongst his faithful friends, continuing the healing he had demonstrated in his brief public ministry before crucifixion, in and through his apostles.

Can "faith healing" be explained? It has often been demonstrated and experienced, but it has never been explained in scientific terms. This does not mean the cures that are attributed to spiritual ministrations are imaginary. Faith is the faculty by which we draw up and live by the unseen realities. The life behind all life is the unseen reality that operates through faith. We can call this invisible energy Perfect Love, but to do so does not explain it. In order to experience the power, there is no need to understand intellectually how the power that heals through faith works. Faith is not a human achievement. It is a gift of God; a gift to the heart, rather than to the head. Healing through faith is not contrary to reason, though it is certainly beyond human understanding.

The whole universe is Perfect Love's creation. Jesus Christ was Perfect Love in incarnation. Holy Communion, Holy Unction, and the laying on of hands are Perfect Love in concentration. All creation is alive with God's life, filled and thrilled with Perfect Love; but the energy of his spirit goes wasted, until we tune in to it as radio and television waves are wasted until a receiving instrument is tuned in to them. Faith is a tuning in to the wavelength of Perfect Love. Perfect Love is the only perfect healing power. As medicine and surgery are the means used by medical science to heal, so Perfect Love is the means used by the Holy Spirit to heal today. Jesus was Perfect Love in perfect focus in the days of his visible ministry, and he is Perfect Love in perfect focus in his continuing presence with and within those who have faith in him today. As they offer themselves as vessels to receive this power and channel it to those in need of healing, they receive and transmit healing.

Faith is taking God at his word. Our Lord, who came to show us what God is like, would not have given the command, "Heal the sick," without giving the power by which this command could be obeyed. He promised that he would be with his followers always. He also promised that they would perform greater miracles when he was no longer "in the flesh" than those which he performed when he was physically with them. He promised that they would lay hands on the sick in his name and that the sick would recover. When we obey him and thank him for keeping his promises, even before we see the results, we exercise faith. When we have the faith which the first apostles had, we achieve, in healing miracles, what they achieved.

Faith is not suggestion. Suggestion is the interaction of the mind over the body. Suggestion is a way of healing: it can be called mental healing, and is as much of God as medical healing, but it is not part of the church's ministry of healing. Faith does not heal. Faith is the key to the power that heals. Faith is our response to the Perfect Love which fills and thrills the universe. Faith is our responsibility, to the extent that it is our response to God's ability. He is able. He offers us his best gift at all times, Perfect Love, his own life, in the unseen form of the Holy Spirit. The gospel is the good news that we have access to Perfect Love, Perfect Light, and Perfect Life that are to be found only in the Living Christ, whatever we call him. Since Pentecost, he has been relevant not only with us; he must also be within us if what he offers is to operate fully. Faith is our response to his offer of himself to us. He does not force an entry into us—he awaits our response to his knock on the door of our personalities. When we open the door of our consciousness to admit him, we exercise faith. When he is within us, our inner "universe" is more wonderful than the outer universe; we have Perfection upon and inside us, touching every part of our nature and drawing body, mind, and spirit toward perfection in healing. Christ's life, received by faith within, banishes fear, dispels dark thoughts, restores lost powers, and vitalizes the body. "Faith healing" is not faith in healing: it is faith in him who heals. There can be no such thing as a small faith in Jesus. Faith in him is always a large faith—enough to meet every need.

The change called "healing" can be instantaneous, as was the case in most of our Lord's healing miracles on the shores of Galilee. However, most often, in our day, the process is gradual, as with the blind man whom our Lord healed; first his sight was blurred, later he saw perfectly. Gradual healing is no less miraculous than instantaneous cure. It is not the length of the time involved in the process that is the determining factor, but the change in the condition of the sufferer from one of sickness to health. Whenever we can say, "It is the Lord's doing, and it is marvelous in our eyes," there is a miracle! When there has been healing through reliance, not on self or human skill but on the undeserved action of God, there is a miracle!

We all tend to take God's blessings for granted; we get so used to natural and medical healing that we do not marvel at them and they cease to seem miraculous. Nowadays we are less inclined to speak of the "miracles" of medical science as scientific knowledge increases and we grow to accept it. Too often we fail to recognize it as "the Lord's doing." We tend to attribute it only to the skill of man. Doctors and nurses are acknowledged as dedicated people. We pray for them and are thankful for them, but it is of the greatest importance that the distinctive nature of the church's ministrations shall not be confounded by any statements which, in our desire to establish good relations with doctors, might nevertheless obscure the responsibility of the church regarding Christ's commission to heal the sick.

Most medical treatment acts automatically. The patient has only to swallow castor oil, and his bowels will be opened! He lies in the operating room and, under an anesthetic, has a malignant growth cut out! He suffers from insomnia, swallows pills, and sleeps! He has a pain in his shoulder and receives a shot, and behold, within hours the pain has gone—no effort, no faith, just the skill of the doctor and the mercy of God.

The danger in man's increasing reliance on medical procedures is that he is becoming spiritually half asleep; while knowledge replaces faith, his faith faculty atrophies. So we are getting what comes from God through knowledge, while we are missing what God offers through faith. "Faith healing," or the church's ministry of healing, as I now call "nonmedical" healing, as practiced by ministers of religion and many of the laity, requires the cooperation of the sick person and of all who are concerned for his healing—relatives, prayer groups, et cetera. Sometimes, perhaps all too rarely, doctors and nurses, in the discipline of their Christian discipleship, give much time to praying for their patients, and I know of a doctor who lays hands on his patients with prayer to build up their faith. The Order of St. Luke the Physician in the United States and many Healing Guilds overseas have as their sole object to recover the faith of Christian people in the power of the risen Christ to do again today what he did nearly 2,000 years ago. We seek, not to downgrade medical science, still less doctors and nurses, but to upgrade the ministry of Jesus Christ as a healer as part of the proper work of the church. Until we look for, in faith, all that there is in him, for healing as well as for sanctification, we remain woefully incomplete. Medication and surgery will increasingly remove symptoms as doctors continue to be (as they ought to be) preoccupied with the diseases people have. But the church must increasingly be preoccupied (as she is not yet) with healing the people who have diseases. Jesus healed people. He made them whole. In offering him to make people whole today, the church is recovering his healing ministry, not as an alternative to medical science or as a useful supplementary ministry, but as a ministry of healing which stands in its own right and which is found to produce results as profound and complete as those recorded in the pages of the New Testament. To be effective, Christian healing must be pursued with the zeal of scientists and Communists!

No part of the human personality is beyond the reach of the Spirit. God wants us to be well. He requires the exercise of faith, the spiritual vision by which we lovingly relate to the living Christ for all he is. Faith is untroubled trust in him—trust without a "but." So many people claiming to be Christians qualify the affirmations of their relationship with God with negations which cancel or greatly reduce a healthy outcome of their religious experience. Often people say, "I believe in God, but the doctor says. . . ." What the doctor says seems more important to them than what is revealed in holy scripture to be the will and the power of God to heal. For them, Jesus might just as well have ignored sick people's bodies, when he ministered to them during his life on earth.

If a person wants to know what medical science can do, he is reasonable and right to go to a doctor to find out. If a person wants to know what prayer and the church's sacraments can do to heal, he is reasonable and right to go to a minister who is dedicated to the church's ministry of healing to inquire what God can do through faith. Not until God's ministers and all who "profess and call themselves Christians" are as zealous in applying "the spirit that raised Jesus Christ from the dead" as doctors are in applying medication will the sick again be healed in our day as they were in the days of the Gospel narratives.

There is certainly a great need for Healing Homes in America. A Healing Home is distinguishable from a general hospital in that the ministry of a priest or pastor is recognized as being at least as important as the ministry of a doctor. No one, it seems, goes into even a church-owned hospital in America for any other reason than to receive medical and nursing help. For sure, it may be that a chaplain will be allowed, even expected, to visit the patient, but after centuries of the church's neglect in offering "healing" in the name of Jesus, it is not surprising that hospitals are not regarded as places where religious healing is practiced. Only when a priest or pastor is in charge, and only if the public knows that the church's healing ministry has priority, will an institution qualify as a Christian Healing Home. After twenty-five years of experimentation in the founding of three Healing Homes in South Africa, the writer knows that there are always doctors, nurses, and occupational therapists who are glad to dedicate themselves to the church's ministry of healing on the staff of a Healing Home. Perhaps less than 10 percent of such professional people know enough or are enthusiastic enough to make such a choice, even if the opportunity were open to them; yet probably as many as 70 percent of the people needing hospitalization would be better treated in a Healing Home than in a hospital. For every hundred occasions that clergy ask the question, "Have you seen your doctor?" when a person complains to them of being unwell, it seems that only once will a doctor ask his patient, "Have you seen your minister?" This is understandable, in view of today's paucity of faith in the means that our Lord used to heal. We get what comes through knowledge; we miss what comes through faith while we are preoccupied with materialism. A mission to the medical profession is needed. Also, Sunday-by-Sunday preaching on the importance of faith in our Lord Jesus Christ for wholeness of life is long overdue in our churches. Every opportunity should be taken by clergy and laity involved in the healing ministry of the church to inform doctors on what the church is again offering to patients, after centuries of neglect in the area of healing. Until more clergy and laity show doctors that they themselves are concerned, not only in spiritually comforting but primarily in healing the sick, doctors will continue to prefer to offer unaided medical science to their patients or, alternatively, to refer them to psychiatrists rather than tell them to consult their ministers. This practice has gone dangerously far in America, in spite of the ever-increasing number of clergy and laity of all denominations now taking seriously our Lord's command: "Heal the sick."

Notes

Chapter 3. Life to the Dying
1. Corrie Ten Boom, *The Hiding Place* (Washington Depot, Conn.: Chosen Books, 1972).
2. Joseph Bayly, *The View from a Hearse* (Elgin, Ill.: David C. Cook Publishing Company, 1969).
3. Alvin Toffler, *Future Shock* (New York: Bantam Books, 1971).

Chapter 6. Faith, Thought, Feeling, and Healing
1. Alexis Carrel, *Man, the Unknown* (New York: Harper & Brothers, 1935).
2. Dr. William Tiller is Head of Material Science Department, Stanford University, California. His statement was made in January 1972 before a gathering of medical people in Phoenix, Arizona.

Chapter 9. Mighty Lourdes and Little Bernadette
1. Michele de Saint-Pierre, *Bernadette and Lourdes* (Image Books, New York: Doubleday, n.d.), p. 227.
2. Zsolt Aradi, *The Book of Miracles* (New York: Farrar, Straus & Giroux, 1956), p. 228.

Chapter 10. The Value of Christian Commitment in the Experiences of Stress and Illness
1. Allen Wyler, Mauda Minoru, and Thomas Holmes, "Magnitude of Life Events and Seriousness of Illness," *Psychosomatic Medicine* 33:115-22 (March-April 1971).
2. William Barclay, *The Letter to the Romans* (Philadelphia: Westminster Press, 1955), p. 11.
3. William Barclay, *Letters of Philippians, Colossians, and Thessalonians* (Philadelphia: Westminster Press, 1957), pp. 95-96.

Chapter 11. Healing and Salvation: A Clinical View
1. Adapted with permission from "Healing and Salvation: Some Research and Its Implications," *Union Seminary Quarterly Review* 24:2 (Winter 1969).
2. Randall Mason, Graham Clark, Robert B. Reeves, Jr., and Bruce Wagner, "Acceptance and Healing," *Journal of Religion and Health* 8:2 (April 1969), pp. 123-42.

Chapter 12. Peeling the Healing Onion
1. Gordon Allport, *Becoming* (New Haven, Conn.: Yale University Press, 1955).

2. "The Meaning of Health," *Religion and Medicine*, ed. David Belgum (Ames, Iowa: Iowa State University Press, 1967), p. 4.

3. Paul Tillich, "Heal the Sick, Cast Out the Demons," *The Eternal Now* (New York: Charles Scribner's Sons, 1961), p. 61.

Chapter 13. Spiritual Healing

1. A paraphrase from the preface to the Ordinal in the Book of Common Prayer. While this chapter inevitably will reflect the theological background of its author, it is hoped that, in these ecumenical days, it will be sufficiently comprehensive to relate to all believing Christians.

2. "Miracle" should not be defined as the violation of natural law but rather as the setting aside of the conditions of one principle or law by the use of another law or principle, e.g., gravity and displacement.

3. This point has been well made in an older book: C. J. Wright, *Miracle in History and Modern Thought* (New York: Henry Holt and Co., 1930).

4. It should be remembered that the earliest account of Mark 3:14-15 gives as a first reason, "That they should be with him"; ability to witness and heal is derived from our relationship with him and not the other way around. See also John 15:5.

5. Evelyn Frost, *Christian Healing* (New York: Morehouse-Gorham, 1940), has an excellent development of this shift in emphasis.

6. See *Journal of the General Convention* (Episcopal Church, 1964), pp. 557 ff.

7. Dr. Large's *The Ministry of Healing* (New York: Morehouse-Gorham, 1959) is a most useful book on the subject.

8. Among them John Rathbone Oliver, Dr. John C. Finney, Moses Lovel, Alexis Carrel, John Hays Holmes, John Graylin Banks, Anton Boisen, Canon Edwin Armstrong, Carl Scherzer, and the Rt. Rev. Wilburn Campbell.

9. If the universe is one, "para-natural" seems a more accurate term than the colloquial "supernatural."

10. As, for example, the Seventy (Luke 10:1).

11. Interesting at the moment is the contrasting resurgence of witchcraft and astrology as well as Eastern mysticism.

12. For example, strictly speaking, is healing a sacrament?

13. The admonition "Honor a physician (Ecclus. 38:1)" will be heeded by the reasonable man who practices Spiritual Healing. There are many God-given healing agents; spiritual therapy is one of them. Not to be certain that the person receiving Spiritual Healing also is under medical care is dangerously close to practicing medicine without a license.

Chapter 16. The Uniqueness of the Gospel in Healing

1. *Los Angeles Times* (1971).

2. Paul Ehrlich, "Eco-Catastrophe!" *Ramparts*, 1969, p. 28.

3. Special Supplement on Mental Illness—"Disturbed Americans," *The Atlantic*, July 1964.

4. "Is the Family Obsolete? Why Kids Blame Parents . . . Why Parents Blame Kids . . . Don't Blame Me! says Dr. Spock . . . Happy Families . . .

'Married' Homosexuals . . . Unwed Couples . . . The Young Revolt That's Rocking the American Family," *Look Magazine* (Special Issue), Jan. 26, 1972.

5. Bryan, Sermon Thesis, "Instant Forgiveness," pp. 173-77, "The Gospel and Its Uniqueness as Therapy for Mental Health," A Dissertation Presented to the Faculty of the California Graduate School of Theology, by G. Edward Bryan, April 1972.

6. Robert B. Reeves, Jr., "Healing and Salvation: Some Research and Its Implications," *Union Seminary Quarterly Review* 24:2 (Winter 1969).

7. Carroll H. Wise, *Religion in Illness and Health* (New York: Harper & Bros., 1942), p. 22. (It would also be well for the reader to note Dr. Messildine's book, *Between Parent and Child*, so he might differentiate between his real parent or the parent within himself in terms of Dr. Eric Berne's transactional analysis.)

8. Bernard Martin, *The Healing Ministry in the Church* (Richmond, Va.: John Knox Press, 1960), pp. 13, 15.

9. Ibid., p. 19.

10. Bryan, op. cit., pp. 173-77.

11. Martin, op. cit., pp. 13-15.

12. Ibid., p. 22.

13. Bryan, op. cit., pp. 177-82.

14. Leslie D. Weatherhead, *Psychology, Religion and Healing* (Nashville: Abingdon Press, 1952), p. 31. Usd by permission.

15. Bryan, op. cit., p. 45.

16. Ibid., p. 48.

17. Ibid., p. 50.

18. See ibid.

19. Jack W. Provonsha, M.D., "Wholeness: An Idea Whose Time Has Come: A Study in Christian Vocation," *Medical Arts and Sciences*, 2nd Quarter, 1959, p. 82. (Some clinics claim 85 percent. I think we'll be safe in saying that while all diseases are not psychosomatic in their origins, there are no diseases without some psychosomatic complications.)

20. William R. Parker and Elaine St. Johns, *Prayer Can Change Your Life* (Englewood Cliffs, N.J.: Prentice-Hall, 1957), and S. L. McMillen, *None of These Diseases* (Westwood, N.J.: Fleming H. Revell Co., 1967).

21. Martin, op. cit., p. 24.

22. Ibid., pp. 31-32.

23. Ibid., p. 36.

24. Ibid., pp. 37-38.

25. Weatherhead, op. cit., p. 38.

26. Ibid., p. 70.

27. Ibid.; also George G. Dawson, *Healing, Pagan and Christian* (New York: Macmillan), p. 147.

28. Weatherhead, op. cit., p. 81.

29. Provonsha, op. cit., pp. 20-55.

30. Weatherhead, op. cit., p. 95. (Though the fact is rarely recognized, hospitals were not first created by the church. They were known in much earlier days in the older civilizations. In Ireland there was one opened in

300 B.C. and in India one in 252 B.C. In Mexico one is known to have flourished before Columbus. Of course, these earlier hospitals depended on the pity of men. The upkeep of hospitals was first taught as a duty when the implications of Christianity were perceived. The word "hospital" first referred to the institutions where hospitality was given to pilgrims on the way to the Holy Land. Many were so ill through the rigors of the journey that they had to stay for long periods. Some were so infirm that they remained until their pilgrim friends called for them on the way back. These older, infirm folk stayed at annexes to the hospitals called "infirmaries.") Provonsha also quotes this same article.

31. Provonsha, op. cit., p. 57.
32. Ibid., p. 58. For further reading the reader may like to see *God and Human Suffering*, by Paul Huback (Glendale, Cal.: Voice of Prophecy), an excellent treatise on the subject referred to here by Provonsha.
33. Carl G. Jung, *Modern Man in Search of a Soul* (New York: Harcourt, Brace & Co., 1933), pp. 263-64.
34. Weatherhead, op. cit., pp. 1-3.
35. Dr. Paul McCleave, address given to White Memorial Medical Center, 1968.
36. Provonsha, op. cit., p. 62. Also, Peter Richey Carter, *Medicine and Man* (New York: Interbooks, 1968), p. 86.
37. Provonsha, ibid.
38. Ellen G. White, *The Ministry of Healing* (Mountain View, Calif.: Pacific Press Publishing Association). Copyright 1909, Mrs. E. G. White.
39. Martin, op. cit., p. 42.
40. Provonsha, op. cit., p. 55.
41. Bryan, op. cit., pp. 177-82.
42. Ibid.
43. Frank W. Kimper, "My Belief in the Reality of Sin" (Professor at Baptist Seminary in Covina, Calif.), p. 1. Unpublished paper.
44. Bryan, op. cit., p. 16.
45. Provonsha, op. cit., p. 59.
46. Ibid., p. 63.
47. Ibid.
48. See W. W. Meissner, *Annotated Bibliography in Religion and Psychology* (New York: Academy of Religion and Mental Health, 1961).
49. Louis Linn and Leo W. Schwarz, *Psychiatry and Religious Experience* (New York: Random House, 1958), pp. 1-5, 7-9, and 11-16.
50. Orville S. Walters, "Metaphysics, Religion and Psychiatry," *Journal of Counseling Psychiatry* 5:4 (1958), p. 50.
51. Ibid., p. 174. Walters quotes A. A. Steinbach from *Can Psychiatry and Religion Meet?* (New York: Basic Books, 1956).
52. James Hillman, *Insearch: Psychology and Religion* (New York: Charles Scribner's Sons, 1970), pp. 1-5.
53. Ibid., p. 6.
54. Leonard Wheelis, *The Quest for Identity* (New York: W. W. Norton & Co., 1958), pp. 92, 100-101.

55. Hillman, op. cit., p. 7.
56. Ibid.
57. Ibid., p. 16.
58. Ibid.
59. Walters, op. cit., p. 243.
60. Ibid.
61. Ibid., p. 244.
62. Ibid.
63. G. Zilboorg, "Some Denials and Affirmations of Religious Faith," *Faith, Reason and Modern Psychiatry*, ed. F. J. Braceland (New York: P. J. Kennedy & Sons, 1955), p. 99.
64. Ibid., p. 246.
65. Mowrer, *Morality and Mental Health* (Chicago: Rand McNally & Co., 1967). It would be well for the reader to read carefully the in-depth articles on medicine and religion; also, part III, "Clergymen, the Cure of the Souls."
66. Robert G. Gassert, S.J., and Bernard H. Hall, M.D., *Psychiatry and Religious Faith* (New York: Viking Press, 1964), p. xiv.
67. L. Nelson Bell, "Evangelists and Modern Psychiatry—The Cost Will Be High If Evangelicals Ignore Study of the Human Personality," *Christianity Today* (Dec. 23, 1966), pp. 21-23.
68. William D. Sharpe, *Medicine and the Ministry* (New York: Appleton-Century-Crofts, 1966), pp. 4, 20, 44, 64.
69. Ibid.
70. Harold Blake Walker, "Why Medicine Needs Religion," *International Surgery*, Sec. 2 (Aug. 1971), pp. 37-40B.
71. Ibid.
72. Ibid.
73. Walters, op. cit., p. 245, quoting Riesman from *Individualism Reconsidered* (New York: Doubleday, 1954).
74. Sharpe, op. cit., p. 60.
75. Gordon Allport, *The Psychological Aspects of Personality* (New Haven, Conn.: Yale University Press, 1953), p. 34. Used by permission.
76. Gordon Allport, *The Individual and His Religion* (New York: Macmillan, 1950), p. 247.
77. Walters, op. cit., p. 247.
78. Ibid., p. 247.
79. Gordon Allport, "The Psychological Nature of Personality," *The Personalist*, No. 34 (1953), p. 347.
80. Walters, op. cit., p. 248.
81. Henry Turkel, M.D., "Outmoded? Has Psychoanalysis Actually Outlived Its Usefulness?" Published privately (Oct. 1962).
82. Ibid.
83. David Shaw, "Quiet Revolution: Freud's Couch Giving Way to 'Now' Therapy," *Los Angeles Times*, February 13, 1972.
84. Mowrer, op. cit., Introduction.

85. Arnaldo Apolito in a paper presented to the Association for the Advancement of Psychoanalysis in New York on January 28, 1970.
86. Ibid.
87. Ibid.
88. Ibid.
89. Ibid.
90. Jack L. Rubins, "Religion, Mental Health and the Psychoanalyst" (Assoc. Clinical Professor of Psychiatry, New York Medical College; Director of the Day Care Center, Karen Horney Clinic), p. 128.
91. Paul W. Pruyser, Ph.D., "Assessment of the Patient's Religious Attitudes in the Psychiatric Case Study," *The Vital Balance* (New York: Viking Press, 1963).
92. Walters, op. cit., p. 249.
93. Pruyser, op. cit., p. 288.
94. Linn and Schwarz, op. cit.
95. Ibid.
96. Ibid., pp. 1-5, 7-9, and 11-16.
97. Walters, op. cit., p. 50.
98. Ibid., p. 174. Walters quotes A. A. Steinbach from *Can Psychiatry and Religion Meet?* (New York: Basic Books, 1956).
99. Walters, ibid., p. 250.
100. Hillman, op. cit., p. 246.
101. Abraham Verghese, paper on psychiatry, Christian Medical College, Vellore, India. Quoted in Gassert and Hall, op. cit., p. xiv.
102. Ibid. Quoted in L. Nelson Bell, "Evangelists and Modern Psychiatry —The Cost Will Be High If Evangelicals Ignore Study of the Human Personality," *Christianity Today* (Dec. 23, 1966), pp. 21-23.
103. Sharpe, op. cit., p. 60.
104. Ibid.
105. Ibid., p. 59.
106. Sharpe, op. cit., p. 60.
107. See Lawrence F. Peter and Raymond Hull, *The Peter Principle— Why Things Go Wrong* (New York: William Morrow & Co., 1969).
108. Rollo May, *Power and Innocence: A Search for the Sources of Violence* (New York: W. W. Norton & Co., 1972).
109. Ibid.
110. Ibid., quoting Riesman from *Individualism Reconsidered* (New York: Doubleday, 1954).
111. Sharpe, op. cit., p. 60.
112. Walters, op. cit., p. 247. Also, Gordon Allport, *The Psychological Aspects of Personality Personally* (1953), p. 34.
113. Walters, op. cit., p. 247.
114. John H. Hunt, M.A., "Religion and the Family Doctor" (J. Roy Call. Gen. PRACTIT., 1969), p. 199.
115. Linn and Schwarz, op. cit.
116. Bryan, op. cit.

Chapter 17. The Relationship of the Human Spirit to the Holy Spirit in the Process of Healing

1. Edwin Lewis, *The Ministry of the Holy Spirit* (Nashville: Tidings Press, 1954), p. 67.
2. Georgia Harkness, *The Fellowship of the Holy Spirit* (Nashville: Abingdon Press, 1966), p. 164.
3. From *The Holy Spirit in Christian Theology* by George S. Hendry, p. 96. Copyright © MCMLVI and MCMLXV, by W. L. Jenkins. Used by permission of The Westminster Press.
4. Ibid., p. 98.
5. Ibid., p. 117.
6. Wade H. Boggs, Jr., *Faith Healing and the Christian Faith* (Richmond: John Knox Press, 1956), p. 59.
7. John Hick, *Evil and the God of Love* (New York: Harper & Row, 1966), pp. 370-71.
8. William Barclay (ed.), *The Acts of the Apostles* (Philadelphia: Westminster Press, 1957), p. 29.
9. Boggs, op. cit., p. 74.
10. Lycurgus M. Starkey, Jr., *The Holy Spirit at Work in the Church* (Nashville: Abingdon Press, 1965), p. 110.
11. Richard K. Young and Albert L. Meiburg, *Spiritual Therapy* (New York: Harper & Brothers, 1960), p. 9.
12. Robert B. Reeves, Jr., paper presented as a lecture at North Carolina Memorial Hospital in Chapel Hill, North Carolina.
13. Mim Randolph Edmonds, "Tell Me Who You Are and I'll Tell You Where You'll Ache," *Glamour* Magazine (Apr. 1970), p. 62.
14. Ibid., pp. 62 and 63.
15. Young and Meiburg, op. cit., p. 11.
16. J. Burnett Rae, in D. Caradog Jones, *Spiritual Healing* (London: Longmans, Green and Co., 1955), p. 138. Used by permission.
17. Ibid., p. 133.

Chapter 18. The Experience of Healing Prayer
1. From the hymn "Immortal Love, Forever Full" by John Greenleaf Whittier.

Contributors

Rabbi David B. Alpert, Chaplain
Jewish Memorial Hospital
Roxbury, Massachusetts

Margaret E. Armstrong, R.N.,
  M.S., Ph.D.
Rochester, New York

Sister Mary Joseph Brewer, R.S.M.
St. Joseph's Hospital
Asheville, North Carolina

The Rt. Rev. Allen W. Brown, D.D.
Bishop of the Diocese of Albany
The Episcopal Church
Albany, New York

The Rev. G. Edward Bryan, Ph.D.,
Senior Chaplain
Glendale Adventist Hospital
  and Assistant Professor
  of Religion
Pacific Union College
Glendale, California

Karla Cooper, R.N.
Midland, Michigan

Judith Correnti, R.N.
Director of the Visiting Nurses
  Association
North Weymouth, Massachusetts

Doris V. Douds, R.N., B.S.
Hospital Nursing Supervisor
Ripley, New York

Florence R. Durkee, R.N., M.A.
Director of Nursing Service
St. Joseph Mercy Hospital
Clinton, Iowa

Glenn R. Frye, M.D. (died August
  1973)
Richard Baker Hospital
Hickory, North Carolina

The Rev. George Lee Gray, Chaplain
Veterans Administration Hospital
Oteen, North Carolina

Imogene Kaserman, R.N.
Supervisor, Lonos Hall
Knoxville General Hospital
Knoxville, Tennessee

Lowell H. Mays,
  Visiting Associate Professor
Center for Health Sciences
University of Wisconsin
Madison, Wisconsin

Jean R. Miller, R.N., M.A.
Rochester, New York

Balfour M. Mount, M.D.
Assistant Professor Surgery
  (Urology)
McGill University Faculty of
  Medicine
Montreal, Canada

The Rev. John E. Pennington, Jr.,
  Pastor
First Baptist Church
Jacksboro, Tennessee

The Rev. Canon H. L. Puxley
The Ecumenical Institute of Canada
Toronto, Canada

The Rev. Robert B. Reeves, Jr.,
  Chaplain
The Presbyterian Hospital
Columbia-Presbyterian Medical
  Center
New York, New York

David John Roche, R.N., A.D.Sci.
Instructor in Medical-Surgical
  Nursing
St. Louis Municipal School of
  Nursing
St. Louis, Missouri

Cynthia A. White, R.N., M.A.
Clinical Coordinator for Nursing
General Medical Service
Presbyterian Hospital
New York, New York

The Rev. Edward Winckley, O.S.L.
Founder, Healing Homes of Africa
Tacoma, Washington